Jenny Craig's™

NO DIET REQUIRED

RECIPES FOR HEALTHY LIVING

Jenny Craig's

No Diet Required

RECIPES FOR HEALTHY LIVING

Oxmoor House®

Library of Congress Catalog Card Number: 97-65133
ISBN: 0-8487-1600-0

Manufactured in the United States of America
First Printing 1997

Be sure to check with your health-care provider before making
any changes in your diet.

Editor-in-Chief: Nancy Fitzpatrick Wyatt
Senior Foods Editor: Katherine M. Eakin
Senior Editor, Editorial Services: Olivia Kindig Wells
Art Director: James Boone

Jenny Craig's No Diet Required

Editor: Cathy A. Wesler, R.D.
Contributing Editors: Jan Strode, Lisa Talamini Jones, R.D.
Designer: Teresa Kent
Copy Editor: Keri Bradford Anderson
Editorial Assistant: Stacey Geary
Director, Test Kitchens: Kathleen Royal Phillips
Assistant Director, Test Kitchens: Gayle Hays Sadler
Test Kitchen Home Economists: Molly Baldwin, Susan Hall Bellows,
    Julie Christopher, Michele Brown Fuller, Natalie E. King,
    Elizabeth Tyler Luckett, Jan Moon, Iris Crawley O'Brien, Jan A. Smith
Senior Photographer: Jim Bathie
Photographers: Ralph Anderson, Van Chaplin, Brit Huckabay, Lee Isaacs,
    Louis Joyner, Juanita Martinez, Howard L. Puckett, Bruce Roberts,
    Charles Walton IV
Senior Photo Stylist: Kay E. Clarke
Photo Stylists: Virginia R. Cravens, Cindy Manning Barr, Christy Flowers,
    Bob Gager
Publishing Systems Administrator: Rick Tucker
Production and Distribution Director: Phillip Lee
Associate Production Manager: Vanessa Cobbs Richardson

Cover: Pizza Milanese (page 129); Mexican Chili-Cheese Burgers (page 212)
    and Chili Fries (page 200); Lemon Cream Pie (page 109)
Back Cover: Jenny with granddaughters Addison and Alexandra

Dedication

This book is dedicated to those special individuals—the clients whom I and all our Jenny Craig employees have had the pleasure to meet over the years. Thank you for making as much a difference in my life as I've hopefully made in yours.

And to my dear friends, the Tuesday Group—Billie Koyl, Sonya Wilson, Jan Amende, and Bettan Laughlin—who have, through the years, enhanced the seasons of my life.

Contents

Introduction   9

The Joy of Healthy Living   11

Menus Through the Seasons   29
Spring   31
Summer   43
Autumn   53
Winter   63

Year-Round Recipes   75
Appetizers and Beverages   77
Breads   89
Desserts   101
Meatless Main Dishes   119
Meats, Poultry, and Seafood   137
Salads and Dressings   167
Side Dishes   185
Soups and Sandwiches   203

Appendices   215
Recipe Index   218
Subject Index   223
Acknowledgments   224

Dear Readers,

For the past 14 years I have had the great personal satisfaction of helping people shed pounds and inches that had been weighing them down for years. It has been inspiring to see the dramatic physical changes that occur when people have the tools to manage their weight successfully. And it has been exhilarating to watch the inner changes that occur as well. Week by week, for every lost pound by a client, there has been a gain—in self-control, self-respect, and self-love. These are some of the most important benefits by which I measure the success of the Jenny Craig Program.

Nearly 50 pounds ago, I changed my own life after a difficult pregnancy. I learned firsthand that taking charge of how I treated my body could be an amazing journey in self-discovery. It's a journey I invite you to take for yourself.

If you want to manage your weight effectively or just to start living a little healthier, realize that the first step is self-awareness. Keep a log of how you feel and what you eat each day; it will give you amazing insights into your habits and attitudes. Strengthen some, discard others. Set goals that are realistic for you, focus on the positive feelings you get when you reach those goals, and start taking little steps to reach them today.

This book is not about depriving yourself of anything. It's about adding the joy of eating deliciously and healthfully to everyday living. It's about taking the time to eat mindfully and to enjoy every minute of it. With this book, you'll begin to savor the sweetness of seasonal fruits, relish the crunch of crisp vegetables and whole grains, and discover the subtleties of fresh herbs and spices. Each of the recipes in this cookbook emphasizes ease, convenience, and healthy living.

As you indulge in the zest for living that comes with the conscious act of eating well, you can begin to experience the pleasure of being physically active. Turn off the TV, and gather with friends who support your new lifestyle. Use exercise not just as a way to burn calories, but also as a release and an opportunity to recharge. Listen to the voice that says "relax," and look to quiet walks, good books, or even a bubble bath for replenishment.

To create a lifestyle that will nurture both your mind and body, know yourself, find new ways to meet your needs, and make new choices. Tap into all the resources you have available—information about nutrition, exercise, and behavioral strategies, and your own inner wisdom. You can rewrite your own story, just as our testimonial clients have.

Try to recommit to taking care of yourself every single day. Always reward your changes, however small. And remember that life is a gift. Celebrate it to the fullest!

Jenny Craig

The Joy of Healthy Living

Balance in All Things   14

The Natural Beauty of Food   16

Celebrate with Flavorful Herbs   18

Exercising New Options   22

De-Stress with Self-Care   24

Profiles in Healthy Living   26

The Joy of Healthy Living

Frustrated with years of unsuccessful dieting? Confused by the ever-conflicting mounds of health information you hear and read each day? You're not alone. In fact, you've probably noticed a backlash against all of the complicated scientific advice, restrictive diets, and punishing exercise regimens of the past.

Most people want to be well and want to improve their health. But today, few are willing to struggle on a daily basis to achieve a "perfect" body. Attitudes about weight management and health are gradually changing. And that's good news, because health and beauty come in a variety of shapes and sizes. You no longer have to be confused or frustrated about healthy living. Just focus on balance and moderation in your daily choices. Once you begin to do that, you'll find that living well can be a real pleasure.

Diet No More

Dieting isn't required to manage your weight—it can actually get in the way of your weight-loss goals. When you diet, you don't learn to understand your body's natural hunger signals. You may gain self-control, but you lose self-awareness because you never learn what really fuels your food choices. And because dieting labels certain foods as forbidden, you can end up feeling deprived, always just a step or two away from abandoning your diet and starting all over again.

To manage weight successfully, you begin with self-awareness. Start by recognizing that there are no "good" foods or "bad" foods; instead, look at weight management as a series of food choices.

In business, successful self-managers embark on a journey. They set goals, make plans, and learn from their choices. They don't deprive themselves; they nurture themselves. You can use this same theory for improving your health and for managing your weight. Then instead of creating a vicious weight-loss, weight-gain cycle, you create a healthy lifestyle.

By becoming a successful self-manager, you discover the joy of healthy living. Nutrition becomes more than a lesson in food groups and fat grams. It grows to include the pleasure, the presentation, the rituals of eating. And exercise becomes more than a way to burn fat and build muscle. It bridges the space between your mind and body, reducing stress, sharpening your thoughts, and increasing your sense of well-being.

Balance in All Things

Face it—life can be hectic and complicated. The daily pressure of meeting both personal and professional demands can get in the way of your best intentions to keep a healthy lifestyle. You may be eating healthier, but can't find the time to exercise. Perhaps you're exercising regularly, but eating erratically. Or you may feel tremendously stressed by trying to "do it all" all the time. The key to better living is to strike a balance among healthful eating, physical activity, and a positive attitude. Finding that balance takes some thought and effort, but the rewards are definitely worth it.

Moderation Is Key

Taking an all-or-nothing approach to your lifestyle doesn't work. Trying to be in total control by *always* eating healthfully and *always* exercising daily is a sure setup for a slip. On the other hand, being totally out of control with your choices and habits won't make you any healthier either.

The place to be is on middle ground, where you eat healthfully and are physically active on most days. It's progress, not perfection, that works in the real world.

Weighing Your Choices

When it comes to tools for healthy eating, remember that food labeling is helpful; labeling food is not. It's important to know how many grams of fat are in a food so that you can track your choices, not eliminate that food all together. This is another example of creating balance and moderation in your lifestyle. When you balance low-fat food choices with an occasional indulgence, you stay on middle ground.

One of the secrets to successful weight management lies at the foot of a pyramid, the **Jenny Craig Food Group Pyramid**, that is. Similar to the USDA Food Pyramid, the Jenny Craig Pyramid promotes building your meals around low-fat, carbohydrate-rich grains, fruits, and vegetables; serving them with moderate amounts of protein-rich milk, meats, poultry, and fish; and accenting them with small amounts of fats or "sweets."

To help balance your choices on a regular basis, use the **Food Group Exchange Guide** (see page 216). Based on a heart-healthy 20% of calories from fat, the Food Group Exchange Guide demonstrates how to "eat low" on the Pyramid.

Jenny Craig Food Group Pyramid

Having It All

Healthy eating isn't about limiting your options. In fact, by balancing your food choices, you widen your possibilities. This book is brimming with lightened family favorites, casseroles, and seemingly decadent desserts. By enjoying these light foods on a regular basis, you'll make room for the occasional splurge.

There are a variety of ways to reduce the fat in all your cooking. Try one or two of the tips listed in the box below, and you'll be amazed at the calories and fat you can save without anyone knowing the difference!

FAT-SAVING TIPS

- Trim all visible fat from meats and poultry before cooking. Remove the skin from poultry before eating.
- Decrease or omit oil from marinades for meats, fish, and poultry by substituting broth or water.
- Decrease the fat in cooking by eliminating added fat (such as cooking oil or butter), decreasing the amount of fat called for in a recipe, and sautéing in nonstick skillets or regular skillets coated with vegetable cooking spray.
- Microwave vegetables, fruit, fish, poultry, and some meats to preserve flavor, texture, color, and nutrients with little or no added fat. Broil and roast meats, poultry, and fish on a rack in a broiler pan to allow fat to drip away.
- Cook tough cuts of meat slowly by braising or stewing. Be sure to remove fat from the drippings (as described below) before using in gravies and sauces.
- Use a fat skimmer or fat-separating cup to remove fat from meat drippings or soup stock. Or chill the meat drippings, and skim off any hardened fat.
- Season grains, legumes, and pasta with herbs instead of high-fat ingredients like gravy, butter, or creamy sauces, which can turn healthy foods into calorie- and fat-laden ones.

The Natural Beauty of Food

The smoothest peach, the reddest pepper, the tartest apple. All reflect the beauty of the seasons. By planning your meals around the fruits and vegetables of the season, your plate can reflect a constantly changing palette of colors and flavors. For instance, switching from crookneck (yellow) squash in the summer to acorn squash in the winter gives a brand-new face to accompany plain roasted chicken. Whether you pick an icy wedge of watermelon or a perfectly poached pear, you can create an entirely different mood just by changing your choices. Seasonal fruits and vegetables allow you to experience an endless array of tastes, textures, and nutrients to nourish your body and soul.

Indulge in the Pleasure of Eating

These days, many of us eat on the run. For families with conflicting work, school, and social schedules, it's a challenge for everyone to meet at the table for a "real" meal. You may not be able to have a sit-down dinner every night. However, making the time for even a quick bite together is a way to relax and reconnect with your family and friends.

Remember that healthy eating is about balance and moderation. Fat-free doesn't mean calorie-free, so it is still important to be aware of the size and number of portions you are eating. You may find you are more satisfied by a smidgen of the real thing than by an ample portion of the fat-free version.

Healthy & Quick Meals

Healthy eating doesn't have to be complicated or time-consuming. Whether it's dinner on the run or entertaining at a moment's notice, you can still do it with style and grace. Consider making just one dish from scratch or trying out a single new recipe or cooking technique. Then accent that dish with prepared items like deli chicken, specialty salad mixes, boxed rices, frozen vegetable combos, or fresh bread from the bakery.

Gone are the days of the carved apple swan and other ornate food garnishes. They've been replaced by practical, natural, and equally attractive accents like lemon curls, herb sprigs, or a single, perfect shaving of Parmesan cheese.

Whether it's an everyday meal or a holiday celebration, you can present it simply and creatively. Throughout this book, you'll find ideas for making every meal special.

Celebrate with Flavorful Herbs

You can reap the physical and psychological benefits of gardening as you add flavor dimension to your foods. Don't dismiss the idea just because you don't have a yard; many herbs will grow prolifically in a pot in a sunny room. But if growing herbs still seems like too much to tackle, most grocery stores carry a variety of fresh herbs cut and ready to use.

Once you start experimenting with different herbs, their novel flavors will keep you hooked. Mundane chicken salad becomes interesting with a sprinkle of licorice-flavored tarragon. A few sprigs of thyme elevate plain roasted pork to elegant heights.

The beauty of these flavorful additions—whether you use fresh or dried herbs—is that you can control the intensity and the combination of flavors. Once you master a few basic guidelines, the cooking canvas is unlimited.

Mixing & Matching Flavors

How much of an herb you add to a recipe is personal preference. But take care with the combinations you try. Flavors can compete or create taste conflicts that ruin an otherwise special recipe. For example, putting two strong-flavored herbs like rosemary (piny taste) and coriander (citrusy, peppery) together results in both flavors trying to dominate. A good rule of thumb with herb cookery is to combine strong-flavored herbs with mild, delicate ones. This will add depth, rather than conflict, to a dish. For a description of herb flavors and suggestions for using them, see the Herb Chart on page 215.

Fresh Versus Dried

Nothing can beat the flavor of fresh herbs. The taste of fresh herbs may be milder than the dried varieties. But because the aromatic oils of fresh herbs are at their peak, flavor nuances are most exquisite when herbs are fresh. To get the most flavor from fresh herbs, snip the leaves with scissors rather than chopping or crushing them with a knife.

Don't go overboard adding too many herbs to a dish. It's much easier to add additional herbs rather than to take some away. That rule goes double for dried herbs, since they are much more concentrated in flavor. When substituting dried herbs in a recipe that calls for fresh, remember to reduce the amount by two-thirds.

DRYING FRESH HERBS

If you have fresh herbs in your garden, here's how to dry them.

- Gather herbs at midmorning, using gardening shears. Cut them just before they begin flowering to capture them at their peak flavors.
- Group long-stemmed herbs, such as rosemary or thyme, in bunches of 10 to 15 stalks. Tie them with string to suspend in air. For herbs with larger leaves, such as basil and cilantro, cut the leaves from the stalks.
- Arrange the leaves in a single layer on a paper towel-lined large screen or on a piece of corrugated cardboard. Place prepared herbs in a dry room with good circulation.
- Be sure herbs are thoroughly dry before you store them (that can take anywhere from two to five days). Snip the leaves from the stalks, and place them in a small bowl. Use kitchen shears to snip them into tiny pieces, or gently crumble them with your hands.
- Place the dried herbs in airtight labeled jars, and store in a cool, dark place.

Hints on Herbs
- To release the fullest flavor of dried herbs, crush them between your palms before adding them to food.
- Store dried herbs in a cool, dry, dark cabinet away from the stove. Heat, air, and light can damage their aromatic oils.
- The flavor of most fresh herbs doesn't hold up during prolonged heating, so the herbs should be added during the final phases of cooking. Bay leaves are an exception and should be added earlier for the flavor to mellow in long-cooking dishes.
- If your bunch of herbs seems slightly wilted, cut off the bottom of the stems, place the bunch in ice water, and chill. Or refrigerate them in a plastic bag lined with moistened paper towels.
- For eye appeal, garnish food with sprigs of the fresh herbs used in the recipe.

Storing Fresh Herbs

In the Refrigerator: Fresh herbs are more delicate than other plants and vegetables. Putting them into the crisper may help, but the best method for preserving fresh herbs is keep them clean, dry, and loosely covered in plastic wrap or plastic bags. If stored in the refrigerator in this manner, parsley can remain fresh up to two weeks. Other herbs typically last seven to 10 days.

In the Freezer: Learning how to freeze fresh herbs can eliminate wasted leftover herbs that would otherwise not stay fresh very long. Freezing can alter texture slightly, but the flavor remains potent. This puts frozen herbs a few notches above dried when it comes to taste.

Herbs can be frozen either whole or chopped. **For whole sprigs**, blanch 5 to 10 seconds in boiling water. Place herbs on paper towels, and allow the herbs to dry thoroughly. Then wrap them tightly in heavy-duty aluminum foil, and freeze. **For chopped herbs**, clean and dry thoroughly; place in plastic freezer bags. Frozen herbs can be added to recipes in their frozen state; no thawing is necessary.

Making Herbed Vinegars

Herb-flavored vinegars can add a jolt of flavor to recipes calling for plain vinegar. They can perk up a variety of condiments like vinaigrettes, slaws, salsas, marinades, and sauces. Sprinkle a flavored vinegar on tomatoes or green beans; or blend it with nonfat mayonnaise, and toss the mixture with chicken or seafood for a salad.

One of most popular herb flavors for vinegars is basil, but for well-rounded flavor, you can try incorporating other flavorings into the vinegar. Just follow these steps:

Step 1: Begin by adding 1 to 2 tablespoons of herb seeds like anise, caraway, celery, cumin, coriander, dill, fennel, or mustard. Then add 1 tablespoon of a whole spice such as allspice, cloves, mace, black or white peppercorns, or star anise. Add 3 to 4 large cloves garlic, peeled. Then drop 1 or 2 dried chile peppers into the bottle.

Step 2: Use a vegetable peeler to remove strips of citrus rind. Insert a few sprigs of any fresh herb into the bottle to keep the rind from sinking to the bottom. Then put the citrus strips into the bottle, using a wooden skewer if necessary.

Step 3: Continue adding any combination of herbs (be sure to use parsley, chives, and bay leaves).

Step 4: Add vinegar at room temperature; heated vinegar will destroy the flavorful oils in the herbs. Use either red or white wine vinegar, rice vinegar, cider vinegar, or other fruit-flavored vinegars. Avoid using sharp, flavorless white distilled vinegar or artificially flavored or colored products. Be sure to go back the next day and top off the bottle with additional vinegar. The level will have dropped, due to air bubbles around the herbs. Let stand overnight before using.

BUNDLING UP FLAVOR

Make your own **bouquet garni** to flavor foods while cooking. Tie 3 sprigs fresh parsley, 1 small sprig fresh thyme, and 1 small bay leaf to a celery stalk with a string of fruit peel. Suspend the bunch in soups, casseroles, stir-fries, or boiling water for cooking vegetables. Remove the bundle before serving. For flavor variations, add sprigs of fresh sage, marjoram, or savory to poultry or pork, and fresh dill or fennel with orange or lemon peel to seafood. Remember, when cooking stews and soups, it's best to add fresh herbs about 10 minutes before serving for the finest flavor.

Exercising New Options

Moderation is also the key to exercise. You might be aware of all the health benefits of exercise, but if it's not fun and doesn't fit your schedule, you won't do it for very long. As it turns out, long, grueling workouts aren't necessary. According to the 1996 Surgeon General's Report on Physical Fitness and Health, moderate exercise is enough to substantially reduce the risk for heart disease, diabetes, colon cancer, and high blood pressure. Accumulating 30 minutes of activity—any activity—over the course of most days can reap real health benefits. The secret to it is finding activities you enjoy and weaving them into your daily routine.

What is moderate exercise? It includes anything from planned activities like walking and weight lifting to fun activities like flying kites and biking with the kids to functional activities like raking and gardening. They all add up to better health and well-being.

Experts say that physical activity also builds your belief in your ability to make changes. And that belief spills over into eating habits. People who exercise regularly tend to eat more healthily.

The Right Combination

As with eating, exercise is about balance. **Aerobic activity** is important for burning calories, losing weight, and strengthening the heart. **Resistance exercise** is important for maintaining muscle and reducing bone loss. **Stretching** helps prevent injury and keeps you flexible. And now, experts are suggesting another component—a **mind-body exercise** such as yoga or tai chi. The best fitness plan includes a balance among all these components.

Exercise A-bout Face

Here's a new way to look at a workout—a 20 minute bout that utilizes "intervals" or short spurts of increased activity to burn extra calories in a short amount of time. Of course, you can't do an entire set of calisthenics in three minutes, but you can focus on a single exercise and alter it each day. For variety, you can adapt the "mini-session" format to almost any activity—walking, jogging, dancing, etc.

Sneaking in Some Exercise

Squeezing fitness into your already busy schedule isn't as hard as you might think. Just seize any opportunity to move around. Here's how:

- •Make the most of your lunch hour. Take a 10 to 15 minute walk inside or outside the office building before eating lunch.
- •Do stretching exercises, do a set of sit-ups, or use an exercise machine at home while you watch the evening news.
- •Take your children (or grandchildren) to the park, and play along with them.
- •Vacuum, dust, and rock 'n' roll. Pop in your favorite tape, and turn your housework into a workout.
- •When you travel, make reservations at a hotel that has a pool or an exercise room; or pack a jump rope and do some jumping before your day begins. On vacation trips, sign up for a walking tour of local attractions and scenic highlights.

Quick Fitness Plan

5 minutes warm-up

1 minute fast pace

2 minutes regular pace

2 minutes fast pace

2 minutes regular pace

5 minutes cooldown

3 minutes resistance

5 minutes stretch

_____

25 minutes

De-Stress with Self-Care

Stress is your body's response to situations. It's the psychological and physiological discomfort you feel when confronted with a challenge like stop-and-go traffic, an increased workload, or a job change. Even the little stresses can add up to deplete you of your energy and positive outlook. To deal with stress, you can choose an unhealthy outlet like overeating, or a healthy one like exercise. Each choice produces vastly different results.

Of course, it's not possible or practical to go on a vacation every time you begin to feel harried. However, a great way to combat stress before it builds to uncomfortable levels is to take care of yourself with a "mini-relaxation."

Incense, candles, books of daily meditations—these items are not throwbacks to the 1960s, but tools for self-nurturing in the 1990s. Though you may not have the luxury of an entire day off, you might be surprised at the replenishment you can get from a quick lunch break outside the office. Even taking a few minutes to look out the window at work or to listen to the birds in the backyard can give you a new perspective on life's everyday challenges.

Although you can never eliminate stress entirely from your life, you can learn to manage it more effectively. One way to do this is to focus on ways to simplify your lifestyle. Here are a few suggestions.

- Reduce your work hours to a manageable load.
- Limit social engagements.
- Combine exercise with family time.
- Plan simpler meals.
- Get help with household chores.
- Go to bed earlier.
- Reduce your "To Do" list to just five tasks.

Conjure up Some Calm

Everyone succumbs to anxiety now and then. Maybe you have the jitters prior to making a speech or an important presentation. Or perhaps you can't get your checkbook to balance. Whatever the reason, don't let stress get to you.

Try "thinking" yourself away from the frustrating situation. Call it a "stress-relief break." Mentally escape for a few seconds to a calm

---

Healthy Indulgences

Candles

Incense

Music

Meditation

Bubble bath

Relaxation exercises

Books

---

environment. For example, visualize watching a beautiful sunset or snorkeling in clear blue water just off a tropical island. Or perhaps your idea of paradise is skiing down the slopes somewhere in the Rockies. Whatever boosts your spirits and takes you away from the everyday grind, try envisioning it.

If daydreaming doesn't work, try muscle relaxation techniques. Alternately tense and relax your muscles, starting from the tip of your toes and ending with your neck and face. When you concentrate on working muscles, you're taking your mind off the stress and placing it elsewhere.

Deep breathing seems to have the same relaxing effect. Relaxing away the stress, however, is more than catching just your breath. True deep breathing requires special attention to the "how" of inhaling air. To start, inhale very deeply through your nose; you'll feel a filling sensation all the way to your abdomen. Hold that breath; then exhale, first from the abdomen and then up through the chest. Repeat five to 10 times for the full effect.

The most important thing is to find what helps relieve your stress and to take a few minutes for yourself. After all, you deserve it.

Profiles in Healthy Living

Before

Breaking the Dieting Cycle

Tom and Robyn Payant knew only too well that weight loss achieved by dieting is often short-lived. For these husband-and-wife partners in a Florida financial services firm, losing excess weight had become a familiar activity—as had regaining the weight they each lost. In fact, Tom had dropped some 30 pounds four different times, only to watch it return when he resumed his old eating habits.

As their combined weight climbed to nearly 360 pounds, they noticed that their clothes no longer fit comfortably, and they had a hard time finding work attire in larger sizes. This time, determined to lose the weight and to keep it off, the Payants enrolled in the Jenny Craig Program. Within four months, they lost a combined 60 pounds. Robyn dropped from a size 18 dress to a size 8, and Tom dropped from a size 44 suit to a size 39.

After

SUCCESS PROFILE

Tom and Robyn Payant

Pounds Lost: 60 pounds combined

Tom and Robyn's Maintenance Tip: Their success lies in applying the same principles used in financial planning to weight management. A balanced portfolio has a variety of investments (cash, stocks, bonds, etc.). Similarly, their nutrition plan includes a balance of different foods.

A Matter of Moderation

For the first time, neither Tom nor Robyn felt deprived while losing weight. It was just a matter of moderation. Learning to plan their food choices and exercising were big parts of their success. As dieters, they had very erratic eating patterns; they were either over-restrictive or overindulgent. But after learning about the variety of easy, low-fat options available, they found out how simple it was to eat healthfully. Regular exercise and tennis also became important and fun parts of their lives.

Partners in Life and in Lifestyle

When it comes to achieving their goals, Tom and Robyn have one special advantage—each other. Not only are they partners in life, but they are partners in lifestyle changes. When they adopted healthier eating and exercise patterns, they became more organized in business management. As a result of this new workstyle, their business is thriving more than ever before.

Old Before Her Time?

For years, Vickie Ortega's body struggled to support what she says was the equivalent of two 40-pound bags of dog food in extra weight. She was only in her 20s, but she had very little energy. (An after-work nap on the couch was part of her daily routine.) She often resorted to food to cope with stress from work and home, and developed back problems related to her weight. When this happened, she knew she needed to do something about her weight, so she called Jenny Craig.

Before

Today, after losing 80 pounds, the 34-year-old mother of two has discovered a whole new energy level. Not only is she off the couch, but she's frequently out biking around the block with her kids. And it's all because of the new attitudes and behaviors she adopted in the process of creating a healthy lifestyle.

After

New Identity and New Control

Vickie says her weight loss has given her a new identity. Before, food used to control her. Now she feels in control of her food choices, and her tastes lean to the natural and unprocessed. Vickie has learned that little things count in big ways. She is proud that every healthy choice she makes for herself and her family adds up to a healthy lifestyle for everyone. And Vickie's family is enjoying every minute of it. She now opts to visit a local fruit and vegetable stand instead of the supermarket. Her children love to snack on mangoes and kiwifruit as much as they do cookies.

Learning to Love Exercise

Exercise is another area in which Vickie has been transformed. Before, Vickie hated exercise—it was something she did only to lose weight. Now she thinks of herself as an active person and exercise as a personal release. After two years of maintenance, Vickie doesn't need a scale to manage her weight. She can tell by a certain pair of jeans if she needs to make an adjustment in her eating or exercise, and she knows the steps to take to get back on track with her goals.

SUCCESS PROFILE

Vickie Ortega
Pounds Lost:
80 pounds
Vickie's Maintenance Tip: When it comes to exercise, Vickie advises to stay within your physical ability and to acknowledge your efforts. Try walking 10 minutes at first; then increase to 15 minutes. If time is limited, break up exercise into mini-workouts. Every little bout burns calories and boosts energy.

A Ladies Luncheon (page 32)

Menus
Through the Seasons

Spring   **31**

A Ladies Luncheon   32

Oscar Night Pizza Party   35

Gardening Get-Together   37

Memorial Day Beach Bash   40

Summer   **43**

Barbecue by the Pool   44

Fourth of July Barbecue   47

Day at the Races   50

Autumn   **53**

Happy Halloween   54

Elegant Autumn Dinner Party   57

A Blessed Thanksgiving   60

Winter   **63**

Christmas Brunch   64

A New Year's Appetizer Buffet   68

After-the-Symphony Supper   72

Whatever the event, from a **Gardening Get-Together** (page 37) to an **Elegant Autumn Dinner Party** (page 57), these menu ideas and recipes are destined to make your favorite occasions unforgettable. With this celebration of seasons, you'll find menu suggestions, a "game plan" for getting the meal to the table, and decorating suggestions for highlighting the occasion.

A Ladies Luncheon (page 32) invites you to dress up the table with linens and china and to arrange a few flowers from the garden in preparation for a midday celebration with your friends.

Memorial Day Beach Bash (page 40) tempts you to take the meal to the water's edge. And don't forget to look for seashells— you'll find that they're useful for creating an icy serving bowl for the shrimp or for serving the cocktail sauce.

A Blessed Thanksgiving (page 60) can bring generations of family members together for a traditional dinner.

Christmas Brunch (page 64) starts the busy day in a relaxed and carefree way. Creole Omelet serves two, but you can easily increase it to serve four or six, depending upon your needs.

A New Year's Appetizer Buffet (page 68) will help you ring in the year with festivity. Decorate a table vibrantly with clocks and bells. Then fill your home with a lively group of friends, and get ready to celebrate at the stroke of midnight.

Spring

A Ladies Luncheon

Grilled Chicken Salad

Honey-Mustard Dressing

Dinner rolls

All-fruit strawberry spread

Brandied Peach Ice Milk

Sparkling water

Meal Plan for
A Ladies Luncheon

- Prepare step 1 of Grilled Chicken Salad; chill at least 2 hours.

- Prepare steps 1 and 2 of Brandied Peach Ice Milk.

- Prepare Honey-Mustard Dressing.

- Complete steps 2 through 4 of salad.

Grilled Chicken Salad

 6 (4-ounce) skinned, boned chicken breast halves
 ¼ cup plus 2 tablespoons reduced-sodium soy sauce
 ⅓ cup honey
 2½ tablespoons sherry
 ¼ teaspoon garlic powder
 ⅛ teaspoon ground ginger
 ¾ pound fresh green beans
 2 tablespoons coarse-grained mustard
    Vegetable cooking spray
 9 cups mixed baby salad greens
 3 medium-size tomatoes, cut into 8 wedges

1. Place chicken in heavy-duty, zip-top plastic bag. Combine soy sauce and next 4 ingredients; pour over chicken. Seal bag, and marinate in refrigerator at least 2 hours, turning occasionally.

2. Wash beans; trim ends, and remove strings. Arrange beans in a steamer basket over boiling water. Cover and steam 11 minutes or until crisp-tender; drain.

3. Remove chicken from marinade. Combine reserved marinade and mustard in a small saucepan; bring to a boil. Reduce heat, and simmer 2 minutes.

4. Coat grill rack with cooking spray, and place on grill over medium-hot coals (350° to 400°). Place chicken on rack; grill, covered, 5 to 6 minutes on each side or until done, basting often with mustard marinade. Cut chicken into slices. Place mixed greens evenly on individual salad plates. Arrange beans, tomato, and chicken over greens. Serve with Honey-Mustard Dressing. Yield: 6 servings.

Per Serving:
Calories 230
Carbohydrate 23.7g
Protein 29.0g
Fat 1.9g
Fiber 3.2g
Cholesterol 66mg
Sodium 479mg
Calcium 67mg
Exchanges:
1 Grain
1 Vegetable
4 Very Lean Meat

Honey-Mustard Dressing

 ¼ cup plus 2 tablespoons plain nonfat yogurt
 2 tablespoons reduced-calorie mayonnaise
 2 tablespoons honey
 1 tablespoon Dijon mustard
 1 tablespoon coarse-grained mustard
 1½ teaspoons rice vinegar

1. Combine all ingredients. Cover; chill thoroughly. Yield: ¾ cup.

Per Tablespoon:
Calories 24
Carbohydrate 3.8g
Protein 0.5g
Fat 0.9g
Fiber 0.0g
Cholesterol 1mg
Sodium 78mg
Calcium 16mg
Exchange:
Free

Brandied Peach Ice Milk

Per Serving:
Calories 173
Carbohydrate 26.1g
Protein 2.9g
Fat 4.8g
Fiber 0.9g
Cholesterol 9mg
Sodium 78mg
Calcium 91mg
Exchanges:
1 Grain
1 Fruit
1 Fat

3 cups vanilla low-fat ice cream, softened
2 tablespoons peach brandy
¼ teaspoon almond extract
1 tablespoon margarine
1 tablespoon sugar
2 tablespoons peach brandy
1½ cups frozen sliced peaches, thawed
¼ teaspoon almond extract

1. Combine first 3 ingredients in a bowl, stirring until smooth. Spoon into a freezer container; cover and freeze until firm.

2. Melt margarine in a medium skillet; add sugar, and cook over medium heat until mixture is bubbly. Add 2 tablespoons brandy and peaches; cook 3 minutes or until peaches are tender, stirring occasionally. Remove from heat; stir in ¼ teaspoon almond extract. Cover and chill.

3. To serve, scoop ½ cup ice cream mixture into each individual dessert dish. Top each with ¼ cup peach sauce. Yield: 6 servings.

Jenny's Tuesday Group—Sonya Wilson, Bettan Laughlin, Denise Altholz (daughter), Billie Koyl—celebrates with a luncheon.

Oscar Night Pizza Party

Party Pizzas

Air-popped popcorn

Antipasto Cups

Meal Plan for
Oscar Night Pizza Party

- Prepare Antipasto Cups, and chill.

- Prepare Party Pizzas.

- As friends arrive, pop the corn, and let the aroma welcome your guests.

Party Pizzas

Per Serving:
Calories 307
Carbohydrate 49.6g
Protein 11.8g
Fat 6.6g
Fiber 3.3g
Cholesterol 6.6mg
Sodium 408mg
Calcium 119mg
Exchanges:
3 Grain
1 Vegetable
1 Fat

4   small round red potatoes
    Olive oil-flavored vegetable cooking spray
1   medium-size purple onion, sliced
3   cloves garlic, cut into slivers
2   (16-ounce) bobolis
6   Roma tomatoes, thinly sliced
2   teaspoons chopped fresh rosemary
2   tablespoons olive oil
    Arugula leaves (optional)

1. Cook potatoes in boiling water to cover 12 minutes; drain. Let cool, and slice each potato into 6 wedges.

2. Meanwhile, coat a nonstick skillet with cooking spray; place over medium-high heat until hot. Add onion and garlic; sauté until onion is tender. Place bobolis on ungreased baking sheets. Coat bobolis with cooking spray; top with tomato, onion mixture, and potato. Sprinkle with rosemary; drizzle with oil. Bake at 450° for 10 minutes. Top with arugula, if desired. Yield: 12 servings.

Antipasto Cups

Per Serving:
Calories 89
Carbohydrate 13.3g
Protein 4.3g
Fat 2.8g
Fiber 3.3g
Cholesterol 5.0mg
Sodium 290mg
Calcium 92mg
Exchanges:
½ Grain
1 Vegetable

12   medium-size sweet red, yellow, or green peppers
 4   medium carrots, quartered and cut into 3-inch strips
24   radish roses
24   green onion fans
12   pepperoncini peppers
 4   ounces part-skim mozzarella cheese, cubed
12   commercial breadsticks

1. Cut a thin slice from the top of each pepper, reserving tops for another use; remove seeds. Cut a thin slice from the bottom of each pepper, if necessary, to help pepper stand upright.

2. Arrange equal amounts of carrot and next 4 ingredients in each pepper cup. Chill thoroughly. Serve each pepper cup with 1 breadstick. Yield: 12 servings.

**Gardening &
Get-Together**

Pitas Niçoise

Sparkling Fresh Fruit Cups

Cranberry-Raspberry Tea

Meal Plan for
Gardening Get-Together

• Prepare Cranberry-Raspberry Tea. Cover and chill, if desired.

• Prepare step 1 of Pitas Niçoise.

• While potatoes cook, prepare step 1 of Sparkling Fresh Fruit Cups.

• Complete steps 2 and 3 of pita sandwiches.

• Just before serving, complete step 2 of fruit cups.

Pitas Niçoise

Per Serving:
Calories 249
Carbohydrate 37.6g
Protein 16.0g
Fat 2.8g
Fiber 6.3g
Cholesterol 19mg
Sodium 492mg
Calcium 60mg
Exchanges:
2 Grain
1 Vegetable
1 Very Lean Meat

½   pound small round red potatoes
⅔   cup nonfat mayonnaise
1   teaspoon dried oregano
1   teaspoon lemon juice
2   large cloves garlic, crushed
3   (6⅛-ounce) cans solid white tuna in water, drained and
    flaked
1   small purple onion, finely chopped
¼   cup Niçoise olives or other small ripe olives, sliced
2   tablespoons red wine vinegar
½   teaspoon freshly ground pepper
4   (6-inch) pita bread rounds
    Red leaf lettuce
4   Roma tomatoes, thinly sliced

1. Cook potatoes in boiling water to cover 10 to 15 minutes or until tender. Drain; let cool to touch, and coarsely chop.

2. Combine mayonnaise and next 3 ingredients, stirring well. Combine potato, tuna, onion, and olives in a large bowl. Sprinkle with vinegar and pepper; toss gently. Stir in mayonnaise mixture.

3. Cut pita rounds in half crosswise; line each half with lettuce and tomato. Spoon tuna mixture evenly into pita halves. Yield: 8 servings.

Sparkling Fresh Fruit Cups

4 medium-size fresh pears, cored and diced
2 tablespoons lemon juice
2 cups halved fresh strawberries
¾ pound fresh plums, pitted and thinly sliced
2 cups peeled, diced fresh peaches
2 cups sparkling apple cider, chilled
   Lemon zest (optional)

Per Serving:
Calories 133
Carbohydrate 33.3g
Protein 1.2g
Fat 0.8g
Fiber 4.8g
Cholesterol 0mg
Sodium 2mg
Calcium 23mg
Exchanges:
2 Fruit

1. Place diced pear in a large bowl, and sprinkle with lemon juice; toss gently. Add strawberries, sliced plum, and diced peach; toss gently to combine.

2. To serve, place 1 cup fruit mixture in each individual dessert cup. Pour ¼ cup sparkling cider over each serving. Garnish with lemon zest, if desired. Serve immediately. Yield: 8 servings.

Cranberry-Raspberry Tea

5 cups water
12 regular-size tea bags
3 cups cranberry-raspberry-strawberry juice blend
¼ cup honey

Per Serving:
Calories 95
Carbohydrate 24.9g
Protein 0.1g
Fat 0.0g
Fiber 0.0g
Cholesterol 0mg
Sodium 7mg
Calcium 8mg
Exchanges:
1½ Fruit

1. Bring water to a boil in a saucepan. Add tea bags; remove from heat. Cover and steep 5 minutes.

2. Remove and discard tea bags. Add juice blend and honey; stir well. Serve warm or chilled. Yield: 8 (1-cup) servings.

The gardening theme provides numerous ideas for decorating. Use a mix of garden flowers and inexpensive garden tools to personalize your table. Gardening gloves can serve as napkin holders, and terra-cotta saucers lined with glass plates can be used for presenting the meal. And don't overlook the idea of moving the table outdoors into the garden for the meal's setting.

Memorial Day Beach Bash

Shrimp Cocktail in Shells

Spicy Slaw

Sourdough rolls

Watermelon wedges

Orange-Lemon Tea

Meal Plan for

Memorial Day Beach Bash

- Prepare ice bowl for Shrimp Cocktail in Shells at least 8 hours ahead.
- Prepare Spicy Slaw. Cover and refrigerate at least 2 hours.
- Prepare step 2 of shrimp.
- Prepare Orange-Lemon Tea.
- Prepare steps 3 and 4 of shrimp.
- Just before serving, cut watermelon into wedges.

Shrimp Cocktail in Shells

Seashells, cleaned and dried
4 quarts water
6 pounds unpeeled large fresh shrimp
2½ cups cocktail sauce
3 tablespoons prepared horseradish

Per Serving:
Calories 195
Carbohydrate 13.7g
Protein 29.4g
Fat 2.0g
Fiber 0.6g
Cholesterol 265mg
Sodium 795mg
Calcium 89mg
Exchanges:
2 Vegetable
4 Very Lean Meat

1. Place a medium-size glass bowl in a large glass bowl. Pour boiling water between two bowls until water comes to ½ inch below rims. Tape rims of bowls together with masking tape. Position seashells in water between bowls. Freeze 8 hours.

2. Bring 4 quarts water to a boil; add shrimp, and cook 3 to 5 minutes. Drain; rinse with cold water. Chill. Peel and devein shrimp, leaving tails intact. Combine cocktail sauce and horseradish, stirring well; set aside.

3. Remove taped bowls from freezer. Pour cold water into medium bowl. Dip large outer bowl into cold water. (Do not use warm water; ice may crack.) Use a kitchen towel to gently remove frozen shell bowl from glass bowls.

4. Place shrimp in frozen shell bowl; set shell bowl in a flat basket or grapevine wreath lined with a plastic bag. (Fill basket with ice, if desired.) Serve with cocktail sauce mixture. Serve immediately. Yield: 10 servings.

Step 1: *Use shells that you collect on the beach for this unique serving bowl. Place shells in water between taped bowls.*

Spicy Slaw

Per Serving:
Calories 64
Carbohydrate 11.7g
Protein 1.9g
Fat 1.9g
Fiber 3.1g
Cholesterol 0mg
Sodium 142mg
Calcium 45mg
Exchanges:
2 Vegetable

8   cups shredded coleslaw mix
1   cup chopped green pepper
1   cup shredded carrot
2/3 cup chopped onion
2/3 cup low-sodium light and tangy vegetable juice
1/4 cup white vinegar
1   tablespoon sugar
1   tablespoon vegetable oil
1   teaspoon chili powder
1/2 teaspoon salt
2   jalapeño peppers, seeded and minced
5   medium-size ripe tomatoes, thinly sliced

1. Combine first 4 ingredients in a large bowl, and set aside.

2. Combine vegetable juice and next 6 ingredients, stirring well. Pour over coleslaw mixture, and toss well. Cover and marinate in refrigerator at least 2 hours, tossing occasionally.

3. To serve, line a large platter with tomato slices. Spoon coleslaw mixture evenly over tomato slices, using a slotted spoon. Yield: 10 servings.

Orange-Lemon Tea

Per Serving:
Calories 82
Carbohydrate 20.7g
Protein 0.4g
Fat 0.1g
Fiber 0.2g
Cholesterol 0mg
Sodium 3mg
Calcium 6mg
Exchange:
1 Fruit

6   regular-size tea bags
3   cups boiling water
1/2 cup sugar
1 1/2 quarts cold water
1   (6-ounce) can frozen orange juice concentrate, thawed and undiluted
1/2 (6-ounce) can frozen lemonade concentrate, thawed and undiluted

1. Combine tea bags and boiling water. Cover and steep 5 minutes. Remove and discard tea bags.

2. Combine tea, sugar, and remaining ingredients, stirring well; cover and chill. Serve over ice. Yield: 10 (1-cup) servings.

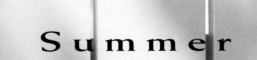

Summer

Barbecue by the Pool

Glazed Turkey Kabobs

Maple-Mustard Carrots

Savory Potato Salad

Cranberry-Wine Spritzers

Meal Plan for
Barbecue by the Pool

- Prepare step 1 of Glazed Turkey Kabobs. Marinate at least 8 hours.

- Prepare step 1 of Cranberry-Wine Spritzers.

- Prepare step 1 of Savory Potato Salad.

- Prepare Maple-Mustard Carrots.

- As carrots cook, complete steps 2 and 3 of kabobs, and step 2 of potato salad.

- Complete wine spritzers just before serving.

Glazed Turkey Kabobs

½ cup apricot nectar
1 tablespoon honey
⅛ teaspoon ground red pepper
1 clove garlic, minced
1 pound boneless turkey breast, skinned and cut into 1-inch cubes
2 medium-size green peppers, seeded and cut into 1-inch pieces
8 large cherry tomatoes
8 medium-size fresh mushrooms
¼ cup no-sugar-added apricot spread, melted
2 tablespoons Kahlúa or other coffee-flavored liqueur
  Vegetable cooking spray

1. Combine first 4 ingredients. Place turkey in a large heavy-duty, zip-top plastic bag; add nectar mixture. Seal bag, and marinate in refrigerator at least 8 hours, turning bag occasionally.

2. Drain turkey, discarding marinade. Thread turkey, green pepper, tomatoes, and mushrooms onto eight 10-inch skewers. Combine apricot spread and liqueur.

3. Coat grill rack with cooking spray; place on grill over medium-hot coals (350° to 400°). Place kabobs on rack; grill, covered, 15 to 20 minutes or until turkey is done, turning and basting often with liqueur mixture. Yield: 4 servings.

Per Serving:
Calories 205
Carbohydrate 22.6g
Protein 26.8g
Fat 1.2g
Fiber 1.5g
Cholesterol 71mg
Sodium 51mg
Calcium 18mg
Exchanges:
1 Vegetable
1 Fruit
3 Very Lean Meat

Maple-Mustard Carrots

1 pound baby carrots, scraped
1½ tablespoons reduced-calorie maple syrup
1 tablespoon reduced-calorie margarine, melted
2 teaspoons Dijon mustard

1. Place carrots in a saucepan; add water to cover. Bring to a boil; cover, reduce heat, and simmer 20 minutes or until tender. Drain well.

2. Combine syrup, margarine, and mustard; stir well. Pour over carrots; toss gently to coat. Yield: 4 (½-cup) servings.

Per Serving:
Calories 57
Carbohydrate 9.5g
Protein 0.9g
Fat 2.1g
Fiber 2.7g
Cholesterol 0mg
Sodium 133mg
Calcium 23mg
Exchange:
1 Vegetable

Savory Potato Salad

Per Serving:
Calories 76
Carbohydrate 16.5g
Protein 2.4g
Fat 0.1g
Fiber 1.3g
Cholesterol 0mg
Sodium 213mg
Calcium 15mg
Exchange:
1 Grain

10	ounces round red potatoes
¼	cup chopped celery
2	tablespoons chopped fresh parsley
1	(2-ounce) jar diced pimiento, drained
¼	cup nonfat mayonnaise
3	tablespoons nonfat sour cream
1½	tablespoons canned low-sodium chicken broth
¼	teaspoon rubbed sage
¼	teaspoon pepper
¼	teaspoon dried whole thyme

1. Wash potatoes. Cook in boiling water to cover 15 minutes or until tender; drain and cool completely. Peel potatoes, and cut into ½-inch cubes. Combine potato, celery, parsley, and pimiento.

2. Combine mayonnaise and remaining 5 ingredients; stir well. Add mayonnaise mixture to potato mixture; toss gently to coat. Cover and chill. Yield: 4 (½-cup) servings.

Cranberry-Wine Spritzers

Per Serving:
Calories 114
Carbohydrate 17.0g
Protein 0.2g
Fat 0.1g
Fiber 0.0g
Cholesterol 0mg
Sodium 22mg
Calcium 9mg
Exchanges:
1 Fruit
1 Fat

1⅔	cups cranberry juice cocktail
1⅓	cups Riesling or other sweet white wine
1	cup sparkling mineral water

1. Combine cranberry juice cocktail and wine in a pitcher. Cover and chill thoroughly.

2. Just before serving, stir in sparkling mineral water. Serve over crushed ice. Yield: 4 (1-cup) servings.

Fourth of July Barbecue

Herb-Grilled Swordfish

Zesty Corn Salad

Tangy Marinated Tomatoes

Vanilla nonfat frozen yogurt with blueberries and raspberries

Meal Plan for
Fourth of July Barbecue

- Prepare Zesty Corn Salad. Cover and chill at least 4 hours.
- Prepare step 1 of Herb-Grilled Swordfish.
- Prepare Tangy Marinated Tomatoes; chill at least 2 hours.
- Complete steps 2 and 3 of swordfish.

Herb-Grilled Swordfish

Per Serving:
Calories 165
Carbohydrate 2.5g
Protein 21.8g
Fat 6.8g
Fiber 0.1g
Cholesterol 43mg
Sodium 277mg
Calcium 14mg
Exchanges:
3 Lean Meat

¼ cup unsweetened orange juice
3 tablespoons minced onion
1 tablespoon chopped fresh thyme
1 tablespoon chopped fresh basil
2 tablespoons low-sodium soy sauce
1½ tablespoons fresh lemon juice
1 tablespoon olive oil
½ teaspoon sugar
⅛ teaspoon salt
⅛ teaspoon pepper
1 clove garlic, minced
6 (4-ounce) swordfish steaks (½ inch thick)
Vegetable cooking spray
Fresh basil sprigs (optional)

1. Combine first 11 ingredients in a large heavy-duty, zip-top plastic bag. Add fish; seal bag, and shake until fish is well coated. Marinate in refrigerator 2 hours, turning bag occasionally.

2. Remove fish from marinade, reserving marinade. Place marinade in a small saucepan. Bring to a boil; boil 1 minute.

3. Coat grill rack with cooking spray. Place rack on grill over medium-hot coals (350° to 400°). Place fish on rack; grill, covered, 3 to 4 minutes on each side or until fish flakes easily when tested with a fork, basting occasionally with marinade. Garnish with fresh basil sprigs, if desired. Yield: 6 servings.

Zesty Corn Salad

4	cups fresh corn (about 8 ears)
1	cup water
1 1/3	cups chopped sweet red pepper
1	cup sliced celery
1/2	cup sliced green onions
1/2	cup chopped fresh parsley
1/2	cup chopped fresh basil
1/2	cup raspberry wine vinegar
1/4	cup sugar
1	tablespoon vegetable oil
1/2	teaspoon salt
1/4	teaspoon pepper

Per Serving:
Calories 165
Carbohydrate 31.4g
Protein 3.8g
Fat 4.8g
Fiber 4.2g
Cholesterol 0mg
Sodium 230mg
Calcium 26mg
Exchanges:
1 1/2 Grain
1 Fat

1. Combine corn kernels and water in a medium saucepan, and bring to a boil. Reduce heat, and simmer, uncovered, 15 minutes or until corn is tender. Drain well.

2. Combine corn, red pepper, and next 4 ingredients in a large bowl. Combine vinegar and remaining 4 ingredients; pour over corn mixture, and toss well. Cover and chill at least 4 hours, stirring occasionally. Toss gently before serving. Yield: 6 (1-cup) servings.

Tangy Marinated Tomatoes

3	large tomatoes, cut into 1/4-inch-thick slices
2	tablespoons sliced green onions
1	tablespoon chopped fresh parsley
1	tablespoon chopped fresh basil
1/4	cup plus 2 tablespoons red wine vinegar
1	tablespoon olive oil
1/2	teaspoon salt
1/4	teaspoon sugar
1/4	teaspoon pepper
1	clove garlic, minced
	Lettuce leaves (optional)

Per Serving:
Calories 55
Carbohydrate 7.8g
Protein 1.3g
Fat 2.8g
Fiber 2.0g
Cholesterol 0mg
Sodium 209mg
Calcium 12mg
Exchanges:
1 Vegetable
1 Fat

1. Place tomato slices in a large shallow dish. Combine green onions and next 8 ingredients in a small jar; cover tightly, and shake vigorously. Pour over tomato. Cover and marinate in refrigerator at least 2 hours. Transfer to a lettuce-lined serving platter, if desired. Yield: 6 servings.

Day at the Races

Roasted Chicken and
Vegetable Salad

Dinner rolls

Glazed Strawberries

Frosty Mint Juleps

Meal Plan for
Day at the Races

- Prepare step 1 of Frosty Mint Juleps up to a day in advance.
- Prepare Roasted Chicken and Vegetable Salad.
- As chicken mixture bakes, prepare steps 1 and 2 of Glazed Strawberries.
- Complete step 2 of mint juleps just before serving.
- Complete step 3 of strawberries.

Roasted Chicken and Vegetable Salad

1	pound fresh mushrooms
8	(4-ounce) skinned, boned chicken breast halves
4	large sweet red or yellow peppers, seeded and cut into 1-inch pieces
2	large zucchini, cut into ¾-inch-thick slices
2	large yellow squash, cut into ¾-inch-thick slices
1	large purple onion, cut into thin wedges
	Olive oil-flavored vegetable cooking spray
½	cup canned no-salt-added chicken broth
¼	cup plus 2 tablespoons balsamic vinegar
3	tablespoons olive oil
2	teaspoons dried rosemary, crushed
1	teaspoon salt
½	teaspoon freshly ground pepper
6	cloves garlic, minced
	Red leaf lettuce leaves (optional)

Per Serving:
Calories 234
Carbohydrate 13.3g
Protein 29.5g
Fat 7.3g
Fiber 3.3g
Cholesterol 66mg
Sodium 375mg
Calcium 50mg
Exchanges:
2 Vegetable
3 Lean Meat

1. Remove and discard stems from mushrooms. Arrange mushroom caps, chicken, and next 4 ingredients in a shallow roasting pan coated with cooking spray. Combine chicken broth and next 6 ingredients. Pour half of broth mixture over chicken mixture.

2. Bake, uncovered, at 425° for 15 minutes. Turn chicken and vegetables; pour remaining broth mixture over top. Bake 10 additional minutes or until chicken is done and vegetables are tender. Cut chicken into 1-inch pieces. Arrange on a lettuce-lined serving platter, if desired. Yield: 8 (1½-cup) servings.

Glazed Strawberries

Per Serving:
Calories 63
Carbohydrate 13.0g
Protein 1.1g
Fat 1.4g
Fiber 2.8g
Cholesterol 0mg
Sodium 1mg
Calcium 21mg
Exchange:
1 Fruit

4 cups fresh strawberries, hulled and divided
½ cup low-sugar strawberry spread
2 teaspoons cornstarch
2 tablespoons unsweetened orange juice
1 tablespoon grated orange rind
2 tablespoons sliced natural almonds, toasted

1. Place 1 cup strawberries in container of an electric blender; cover and process until smooth. Combine puree and strawberry spread in a 1-quart baking dish. Microwave, uncovered, at HIGH 2 to 3 minutes or until mixture begins to boil.

2. Combine cornstarch and orange juice, stirring until smooth. Stir orange juice mixture into strawberry puree mixture. Microwave, uncovered, at HIGH 2 minutes or until thickened; stir in orange rind. Cover and chill.

3. Place remaining 3 cups strawberries in a large bowl. Pour strawberry sauce over berries; toss gently. Spoon mixture into individual dessert dishes; sprinkle with almonds. Yield: 6 servings.

Frosty Mint Juleps

Per Serving:
Calories 93
Carbohydrate 6.1g
Protein 1.9g
Fat 0.5g
Fiber 0.0g
Cholesterol 0mg
Sodium 5mg
Calcium 11mg
Exchanges:
½ Grain
1 Fat

5 cups water
2¼ cups loosely packed fresh mint sprigs
1 cup bourbon
¼ cup plus 2 tablespoons sifted powdered sugar
Crushed ice
Fresh mint sprigs (optional)

1. Combine first 4 ingredients in container of an electric blender; cover and process until smooth. Cover and chill at least 4 hours.

2. Strain mixture into a large pitcher, discarding mint sprigs. To serve, fill glasses with crushed ice; add bourbon mixture. Garnish with mint sprigs, if desired. Yield: 8 (¾-cup) servings.

Autumn

Happy Halloween

Harvest Stew

Mixed salad greens with
fat-free Ranch dressing

Dinner rolls

Autumn Spice Squares

Meal Plan for
Happy Halloween

- Prepare steps 1 and 2 of Harvest Stew.

- As stew simmers, prepare Autumn Spice Squares.

- Complete step 3 of stew.

- Toss salad greens, and drizzle with dressing.

Harvest Stew

1½ pounds top round steak, trimmed and cut into 1-inch pieces
¾   cup chopped onion
½   teaspoon freshly ground pepper
2   cloves garlic, minced
    Vegetable cooking spray
2   (13¾-ounce) cans no-salt-added beef broth
2   bay leaves
1   (14½-ounce) can no-salt-added whole tomatoes,
    undrained and chopped
1½ cups peeled, cubed sweet potato
1   cup peeled, cubed acorn squash or butternut squash
1   cup peeled, cubed red potato
2   teaspoons beef-flavored bouillon granules
½   teaspoon chili powder
¼   teaspoon ground allspice
¼   teaspoon ground cloves
¼   cup water
3   tablespoons all-purpose flour

Per Serving:
Calories 259
Carbohydrate 22.0g
Protein 29.2g
Fat 5.1g
Fiber 1.7g
Cholesterol 65mg
Sodium 395mg
Calcium 73mg
Exchanges:
1½ Grain
3 Lean Meat

1. Cook first 4 ingredients in a Dutch oven coated with cooking spray over medium heat until steak is browned, stirring often. Drain and pat dry with paper towels. Wipe pan with a paper towel.

2. Return steak mixture to Dutch oven. Add broth, bay leaves, and tomato. Bring to a boil; cover, reduce heat, and simmer 1 hour and 15 minutes or until meat is tender. Stir in sweet potato and next 6 ingredients. Bring to a boil; cover, reduce heat, and simmer 55 minutes or until vegetables are tender. Remove and discard bay leaves.

3. Combine water and flour, stirring well. Add to beef mixture; cook, stirring constantly, until mixture is thickened. Yield: 6 (1½-cup) servings.

Autumn Spice Squares

Per Square:
Calories 90
Carbohydrate 14.8g
Protein 1.2g
Fat 3.1g
Fiber 0.5g
Cholesterol 9mg
Sodium 99mg
Calcium 21mg
Exchange:
1 Grain
1 Fat

1½ cups all-purpose flour
1 teaspoon baking powder
1 teaspoon baking soda
½ teaspoon salt
1 teaspoon ground cinnamon
¼ teaspoon ground ginger
⅛ teaspoon pepper
1 egg, lightly beaten
1 cup unsweetened applesauce
⅔ cup sugar
¼ cup vegetable oil
1 teaspoon vanilla extract
1 (8-ounce) can crushed pineapple in juice, drained
3 tablespoons semisweet chocolate mini-morsels
  Vegetable cooking spray
2 teaspoons powdered sugar

1. Combine first 7 ingredients in a mixing bowl; make a well in center of mixture. Combine egg and next 4 ingredients; add to flour mixture, stirring just until dry ingredients are moistened. Stir in pineapple and chocolate morsels.

2. Spoon batter into a 13- x 9- x 2-inch pan coated with cooking spray. Bake at 350° for 20 minutes or until a wooden pick inserted in center comes out clean. Cool in pan on a wire rack. Sift powdered sugar over cooled cake. Yield: 2 dozen squares.

Elegant Autumn Dinner Party

Burgundy Beef

Parslied Fettuccine

Mixed baby greens with fat-free Italian dressing

Crusty French rolls

Cinnamon Cappuccino

Meal Plan for
Elegant Autumn Dinner Party

- Prepare Burgundy Beef.

- As carrot is added to Burgundy Beef, start Parslied Fettuccine.

- Toss greens with dressing.

- Prepare Cinnamon Cappuccino near end of meal.

Burgundy Beef

Per Serving:
Calories 238
Carbohydrate 9.6g
Protein 25.6g
Fat 9.4g
Fiber 1.7g
Cholesterol 70mg
Sodium 94mg
Calcium 39mg
Exchanges:
2 Vegetable
3 Lean Meat

1   cup Burgundy or other dry red wine
2   tablespoons cognac
1   tablespoon black peppercorns
1   teaspoon dried whole thyme
1   teaspoon Worcestershire sauce
2   bay leaves
2   pounds beef tenderloin
    Vegetable cooking spray
1   tablespoon olive oil
6   ounces pearl onions, peeled
1   cup canned low-sodium beef broth
3   medium carrots, scraped and cut diagonally into ½-inch
      pieces
1   (9-ounce) package frozen artichoke hearts
½   pound fresh snow pea pods, trimmed
1   tablespoon cornstarch
1   tablespoon water
¼   teaspoon freshly ground pepper

1. Combine first 6 ingredients in a large heavy-duty, zip-top plastic bag. Trim fat from beef; cut beef into 1-inch cubes, and place in bag with wine mixture. Seal bag, and shake to coat; marinate in refrigerator 8 hours. Drain beef, reserving marinade. Set beef aside. Strain marinade, and set aside.

2. Coat a large nonstick skillet with cooking spray, and add olive oil. Place skillet over medium-high heat until oil is hot. Add half of beef cubes; cook 5 minutes or until browned, stirring often. Remove cooked beef cubes from skillet, and set aside. Add remaining beef cubes to skillet, and cook until browned. Remove from skillet, and set aside.

3. Add onions to skillet, and sauté 5 minutes or until tender. Stir in reserved marinade and beef broth. Bring to a boil; reduce heat, and simmer, uncovered, 15 minutes. Add carrot; cook 5 minutes. Add artichoke hearts; cook 6 minutes. Add beef cubes; cook 5 minutes. Add snow peas; cook 3 minutes or until crisp-tender. Combine cornstarch and water, stirring until smooth; stir cornstarch mixture and ground pepper into beef mixture. Cook until vegetables and meat are tender and mixture is slightly thickened. Yield: 8 servings.

Parslied Fettuccine

8   ounces fettuccine, uncooked
2   teaspoons reduced-calorie margarine
1   tablespoon chopped fresh parsley

1. Cook pasta according to package directions, omitting salt and fat. Drain well.

2. Place cooked pasta in a large serving bowl. Add margarine, and toss mixture well. Sprinkle pasta mixture with parsley. Yield: 8 (½-cup) servings.

Per Serving:
Calories 110
Carbohydrate 21.2g
Protein 3.6g
Fat 1.1g
Fiber 0.7g
Cholesterol 0mg
Sodium 11mg
Calcium 6mg
Exchanges:
1½ Grain

Cinnamon Cappuccino

3½   cups skim milk
½   cup instant nonfat dry milk powder
2   tablespoons plus 2 teaspoons sugar
2   tablespoons Dutch process cocoa
4   cups hot espresso coffee
2   tablespoons plus 2 teaspoons brandy (optional)
    Ground cinnamon

1. Combine first 4 ingredients in a medium saucepan; stir well. Cook over medium heat, stirring constantly, until sugar is dissolved and mixture is thoroughly heated.

2. Combine warm milk mixture and hot espresso in container of an electric blender; add brandy, if desired. Cover and process until frothy. Pour into individual cups, and sprinkle with cinnamon. Serve immediately. Yield: 8 (1-cup) servings.

Per Serving:
Calories 93
Carbohydrate 14.4g
Protein 6.9g
Fat 0.4g
Fiber 0.0g
Cholesterol 4mg
Sodium 99mg
Calcium 231mg
Exchange:
1 Skim Milk

A Blessed Thanksgiving

Turkey Breast with
Cornbread Stuffing

Creamed Pumpkin
Potatoes

Steamed green beans

Holiday Cranberry Relish

Ambrosia

Meal Plan for
A Blessed Thanksgiving

- Prepare Holiday Cranberry Relish the day ahead.

- Start cooking potatoes for Creamed Pumpkin Potatoes.

- As potatoes cook, prepare Turkey Breast with Cornbread Stuffing.

- As turkey bakes, prepare Ambrosia.

- Complete creamed potatoes.

- Steam the green beans during the last few minutes the turkey bakes.

Turkey Breast with Cornbread Stuffing

1 (6-ounce) package cornbread mix
1 egg
²/₃ cup skim milk
1 (3-pound) boneless turkey breast, skinned
Vegetable cooking spray
2 teaspoons vegetable oil
1½ cups finely chopped fresh mushrooms
¾ cup finely chopped onion
1 clove garlic, minced
¼ cup minced fresh parsley
3 tablespoons currants
2 tablespoons chopped pecans
½ teaspoon salt
¼ teaspoon pepper
½ cup unsweetened apple juice
2 tablespoons honey
⅛ teaspoon dried thyme
1 small clove garlic, crushed

Per Serving:
Calories 232
Carbohydrate 18.4g
Protein 27.9g
Fat 6.3g
Fiber 1.1g
Cholesterol 88mg
Sodium 367mg
Calcium 39mg
Exchanges:
1 Grain
3 Lean Meat

1. Prepare cornbread according to package directions, using egg and skim milk. Let cool. Cut into large chunks. Position knife blade in food processor bowl; add cornbread. Pulse 4 times or until coarsely crumbled.

2. Trim fat from turkey; remove tendons. Place turkey, boned side up, on heavy-duty plastic wrap. From center, slice horizontally through thickest part of each side almost to outer edge; flip each cut piece over to enlarge breast. Cover with heavy-duty plastic wrap; flatten to ½-inch thickness, using a meat mallet or rolling pin.

3. Coat a large nonstick skillet with cooking spray; add oil. Place over medium-high heat until hot. Add mushrooms, onion, and 1 clove garlic; sauté 5 minutes or until tender. Stir in cornbread, parsley, and next 4 ingredients. Spoon onto center of turkey, leaving a 2-inch border at sides; roll up, jellyroll fashion, starting with short side. Tie securely at 2-inch intervals with string. Place, seam side down, on a rack in a roasting pan coated with cooking spray. Insert a meat thermometer into turkey.

4. Combine apple juice and remaining 3 ingredients; brush over turkey. Shield turkey with aluminum foil. Bake at 325° for 1 hour; baste often with juice mixture. Uncover; bake 30 minutes or until thermometer registers 170°. Remove string; let stand 10 minutes. Yield: 12 servings.

Creamed Pumpkin Potatoes

Per Serving:
Calories 161
Carbohydrate 26.7g
Protein 4.9g
Fat 4.5g
Fiber 2.7g
Cholesterol 11mg
Sodium 283mg
Calcium 79mg
Exchanges:
1½ Grain
1 Fat

  4 cups (1½-inch) peeled, cubed baking potato (about 1½ pounds)
2¼ cups canned unsweetened pumpkin
  ¼ cup (1 ounce) shredded sharp Cheddar cheese
  ¼ cup low-fat sour cream (at room temperature)
  ½ teaspoon salt
  ⅛ teaspoon ground white pepper

1. Place potato in a large saucepan; add water to cover, and bring to a boil. Cover and cook 30 minutes or until tender; drain.

2. Combine potato, pumpkin, and remaining ingredients, beating at medium speed of an electric mixer until smooth. Yield: 5 (1-cup) servings.

Holiday Cranberry Relish

Per Serving:
Calories 52
Carbohydrate 13.5g
Protein 0.3g
Fat 0.1g
Fiber 1.4g
Cholesterol 0mg
Sodium 0mg
Calcium 11mg
Exchange:
1 Fruit

  1 orange
  2 cups fresh cranberries
  1 cup diced Red Delicious apple
  ⅓ cup sugar
  1 (8-ounce) can unsweetened crushed pineapple, drained

1. Cut unpeeled orange into 4 pieces; remove seeds. Position knife blade in food processor bowl. Add orange, and process until finely chopped. Transfer to a nonaluminum bowl.

2. Place cranberries in processor bowl; process until coarsely ground. Add cranberries, apple, sugar, and pineapple to chopped orange; stir well. Cover and chill at least 8 hours. Yield: 12 (¼-cup) servings.

Ambrosia

Per Serving:
Calories 36
Carbohydrate 9.0g
Protein 0.6g
Fat 0.1g
Fiber 1.4g
Cholesterol 0mg
Sodium 0mg
Calcium 16mg
Exchange:
½ Fruit

  ½ cup unsweetened orange juice
  ¼ teaspoon coconut extract
  3 large oranges, peeled and sectioned
  3 medium-size pink grapefruit, peeled and sectioned
  1 medium-size Red Delicious apple, cored and sliced

1. Combine all ingredients in a bowl; stir gently. Cover and chill at least 1 hour. To serve, spoon fruit mixture into individual dessert bowls. Yield: 12 (½-cup) servings.

Winter

Christmas Brunch

Minted Fruit Compote
Creole Omelet
Herbed Popovers
Orange juice

Meal Plan for
Christmas Brunch

• Prepare Minted Fruit Compote; chill at least 30 minutes.

• Prepare Herbed Popovers.

• While popovers bake, prepare Creole Omelet.

Minted Fruit Compote

3   cups frozen melon balls, thawed
2   cups chopped red apple
2   bananas, sliced
3   tablespoons lemon juice
3   tablespoons finely chopped fresh mint
2   kiwifruit, peeled and sliced
    Fresh mint sprigs (optional)

Per Serving:
Calories 103
Carbohydrate 25.1g
Protein 1.5g
Fat 0.7g
Fiber 4.1g
Cholesterol 0mg
Sodium 8mg
Calcium 21mg
Exchange:
1 Fruit

1. Combine first 3 ingredients in a large bowl; toss gently. Add lemon juice and chopped mint. Cover and chill at least 30 minutes. Add kiwifruit, and toss gently. Garnish with mint sprigs, if desired. Yield: 6 (1-cup) servings.

Jenny and husband Sid celebrate the holidays with their grandchildren.

Creole Omelet

Creole Omelet

Per Serving:
Calories 191
Carbohydrate 19.7g
Protein 10.0g
Fat 8.5g
Fiber 2.8g
Cholesterol 221mg
Sodium 436mg
Calcium 116mg
Exchanges:
1 High-Fat Meat
1 Grain
1 Vegetable

1   teaspoon vegetable oil
1   teaspoon all-purpose flour
½   cup thinly sliced onion
½   cup thinly sliced green pepper
½   cup thinly sliced celery
½   teaspoon dried thyme
1   clove garlic, minced
¼   cup canned no-salt-added chicken broth
1   (14½-ounce) can no-salt-added whole tomatoes,
      drained and chopped
¼   teaspoon salt
2   eggs, separated
1   tablespoon skim milk
1   tablespoon all-purpose flour
      Dash of pepper
      Vegetable cooking spray

   1. Place oil in a medium nonstick skillet. Add 1 teaspoon flour;
stir until smooth. Cook over medium heat until caramel colored,
stirring often. Add onion and next 4 ingredients, and sauté over
medium-high heat 4 minutes. Add broth, and cook until thick and
bubbly, stirring often. Stir in tomato and salt. Set aside; keep warm.

2. Beat egg yolks in a small bowl at high speed of an electric mixer until thick and pale. Add milk, and beat until blended; set aside.

3. Beat egg whites at high speed of mixer until soft peaks form. Gradually add 1 tablespoon flour and dash of pepper, beating until stiff peaks form. Fold egg white mixture into yolk mixture.

4. Coat a nonstick skillet with cooking spray, and place over medium heat until hot. Pour egg mixture into skillet, spreading evenly. Reduce heat, and cook 8 minutes or until just set. Loosen omelet with a spatula; fold in half. Slide onto a serving platter. Spoon tomato mixture over omelets, cut in half, and serve immediately. Yield: 2 servings.

Note: This recipe can be doubled or tripled for 4 or 6 servings, if desired. Just be sure to cook the egg mixture in batches.

Herbed Popovers

1	cup bread flour
1	cup skim milk
2	eggs, lightly beaten
2	egg whites
1	tablespoon reduced-calorie stick margarine, melted
1	teaspoon dried basil
1	teaspoon dried oregano
1	teaspoon dried thyme
1/2	teaspoon freshly ground pepper
1/4	teaspoon salt
	Vegetable cooking spray

Per Popover:
Calories 141
Carbohydrate 19.4g
Protein 7.5g
Fat 3.6g
Fiber 0.6g
Cholesterol 74mg
Sodium 177mg
Calcium 76mg
Exchanges:
1 Grain
1 Fat

1. Combine all ingredients except cooking spray in a medium bowl; stir with a wire whisk until smooth.

2. Pour batter into popover pan cups coated with cooking spray. Place in a cold oven.

3. Turn oven on 450°; bake 15 minutes. Reduce heat to 350°; bake 35 additional minutes or until crusty and brown. Serve immediately. Yield: 6 popovers.

A New Year's Appetizer Buffet

Smoked Salmon Pâté

Black-Eyed Caviar

Broccoli Quiche Bites

Mushroom Phyllo Bundles

Tortellini Toss

Meal Plan for
A New Year's Appetizer Buffet

- Prepare Black-Eyed Caviar a day ahead.

- Prepare Smoked Salmon Pâté. Cover and chill.

- Prepare Tortellini Toss.

- Before guests arrive, prepare Mushroom Phyllo Bundles, but don't bake. Place bundles on baking sheet. Cover with a damp towel until ready to bake.

- Prepare Broccoli Quiche Bites.

Smoked Salmon Pâté

¼   pound smoked salmon

2   tablespoons minced onion

2   tablespoons low-fat sour cream

1   tablespoon minced fresh chives

1   tablespoon dried dillweed

⅛   teaspoon ground white pepper

4   to 5 drops of hot sauce

½   (8-ounce) package Neufchâtel cheese

Per Tablespoon:
Calories 24
Carbohydrate 0.4g
Protein 1.7g
Fat 1.8g
Fiber 0.0g
Cholesterol 6mg
Sodium 68mg
Calcium 10mg
Exchange:
Free

1. Position knife blade in food processor bowl; add all ingredients. Process until smooth. Chill; serve with crackers. Yield: 1¼ cups.

Black-Eyed Caviar

1   (16-ounce) package frozen black-eyed peas

½   cup diced sweet red pepper

½   cup sliced green onions

¼   cup minced fresh cilantro or parsley

3   tablespoons cider vinegar

3   tablespoons commercial fat-free Italian dressing

¼   teaspoon salt

¼   teaspoon hot sauce

⅛   teaspoon pepper

1   clove garlic, minced

Per Tablespoon:
Calories 12
Carbohydrate 2.3g
Protein 0.8g
Fat 0.1g
Fiber 0.2g
Cholesterol 0mg
Sodium 20mg
Calcium 7mg
Exchange:
Free

1. Cook peas according to package directions, omitting salt and fat; drain. Combine peas, red pepper, and remaining ingredients. Cover; chill at least 8 hours. Serve with pita chips. Yield: 3½ cups.

Broccoli Quiche Bites

Per Appetizer:
Calories 39
Carbohydrate 0.6g
Protein 2.7g
Fat 2.8g
Fiber 0.1g
Cholesterol 64mg
Sodium 40mg
Calcium 53mg
Exchange:
1 Fat

Vegetable cooking spray
1 teaspoon olive oil
¾ cup finely chopped fresh broccoli
¼ cup finely chopped sweet red pepper
1 clove garlic, minced
4 eggs, separated
½ cup (2 ounces) finely shredded Swiss cheese
3 tablespoons grated Parmesan cheese
½ teaspoon dried basil
⅛ teaspoon ground red pepper

1. Coat a large nonstick skillet with cooking spray. Add oil; place over medium-high heat until hot. Add broccoli, chopped pepper, and garlic; sauté until crisp-tender.

2. Combine egg yolks and remaining 4 ingredients in a medium bowl; stir well. Beat egg whites in a large bowl until stiff but not dry; gently fold into yolk mixture. Gently fold in broccoli mixture.

3. Spoon 1 tablespoon broccoli mixture into each of 32 miniature (1¾-inch) muffin cups coated with cooking spray. Bake at 425° for 10 minutes or until set. Cool in pans 1 minute. Remove from pans, and serve immediately. Yield: 1½ dozen appetizers.

Mushroom Phyllo Bundles

Per Bundle:
Calories 26
Carbohydrate 2.0g
Protein 0.4g
Fat 1.7g
Fiber 0.1g
Cholesterol 0mg
Sodium 26mg
Calcium 2mg
Exchange:
Free

2 tablespoons blanched slivered almonds, toasted
Butter-flavored vegetable cooking spray
2½ cups chopped fresh mushrooms
1 clove garlic, crushed
2 tablespoons nonfat mayonnaise
¼ teaspoon dried thyme
Dash of ground white pepper
3 sheets frozen phyllo pastry, thawed
Blanched whole chives (optional)

1. Place almonds in container of an electric blender. Cover and process until ground; set aside.

2. Coat a large nonstick skillet with cooking spray; place over medium-high heat until hot. Add mushrooms and garlic; sauté until mushrooms are tender and liquid evaporates. Stir ground almonds, mayonnaise, thyme, and pepper into mushroom mixture; stir well.

3. Place 1 sheet phyllo on a damp towel (keep remaining phyllo covered). Lightly coat phyllo with cooking spray. Layer remaining 2 sheets phyllo on first sheet, lightly coating each with cooking spray. Cut stack of phyllo into 18 (3-inch) squares, using a sharp knife.

4. Spoon about 2 teaspoons mushroom mixture into center of each phyllo square. Pull corners of phyllo over filling, and gently twist to close pastry. Lightly spray with cooking spray. Place on an ungreased baking sheet. Repeat procedure with remaining phyllo squares and mushroom mixture. Bake at 350° for 12 minutes or until golden. Tie a blanched chive around each bundle, if desired. Yield: 1½ dozen bundles.

Tortellini Toss

1	tablespoon fennel seeds
2	teaspoons cumin seeds
2	pounds fresh cheese-filled spinach tortellini, uncooked
4	ounces unsliced Canadian bacon, cut into ¾-inch cubes
1	large sweet yellow or red pepper, seeded and cut into 1-inch pieces
¼	cup sliced ripe olives, drained
½	cup commercial fat-free Italian dressing
3	large cloves garlic, sliced
1	pint cherry tomatoes, halved

Per Serving:
Calories 194
Carbohydrate 29.6g
Protein 11.2g
Fat 3.6g
Fiber 0.3g
Cholesterol 4mg
Sodium 410mg
Calcium 143mg
Exchanges:
1 Grain
1 Lean Meat

1. Cook fennel and cumin seeds in a skillet over medium heat until seeds are lightly browned and fragrant, shaking skillet often. Remove seeds from heat, and cool.

2. Cook tortellini according to package directions, omitting salt and fat; drain. Combine tortellini, seeds, Canadian bacon, pepper, and olives in a large serving bowl. Combine Italian dressing and garlic; drizzle over tortellini mixture. Toss well. Gently stir in tomatoes. To serve, provide long wooden skewers for spearing. Yield: 16 appetizer servings.

Meal Plan for
After-the-Symphony Supper

• Prepare Individual Lime Cheesecakes up to a day in advance.

• Prepare Crabmeat Imperial.

• As crabmeat bakes, drizzle mixed baby greens with vinaigrette.

Crabmeat Imperial

Vegetable cooking spray
½ cup chopped celery
1 cup chopped sweet red or green pepper
2 tablespoons chopped fresh parsley
1 teaspoon prepared mustard
⅛ teaspoon ground white pepper
⅛ teaspoon ground red pepper
⅛ teaspoon hot sauce
2 eggs, lightly beaten
⅓ cup reduced-calorie mayonnaise
2 pounds fresh lump crabmeat, drained and flaked

Per Serving:
Calories 153
Carbohydrate 2.2g
Protein 21.4g
Fat 6.0g
Fiber 0.5g
Cholesterol 125mg
Sodium 1190mg
Calcium 73mg
Exchanges:
3 Lean Meat

1. Coat a nonstick skillet with cooking spray; place over medium-high heat until hot. Add celery and chopped pepper; sauté until tender. Remove from heat; stir in parsley and next 4 ingredients. Combine eggs and mayonnaise; stir with a wire whisk until smooth. Stir in celery mixture; add crabmeat, stirring gently. Spoon into baking shells; place on a baking sheet. Bake at 375° for 20 minutes. Yield: 8 servings.

Individual Lime Cheesecakes

12 vanilla wafers
¾ cup 1% low-fat cottage cheese
1 (8-ounce) package Neufchâtel cheese, softened
¼ cup plus 2 tablespoons sugar
1 tablespoon grated lime rind
1 tablespoon lime juice
1 teaspoon vanilla extract
2 eggs
¼ cup vanilla low-fat yogurt
2 medium kiwifruit, peeled, sliced, and halved

Per Serving:
Calories 127
Carbohydrate 11.9g
Protein 5.3g
Fat 6.5g
Fiber 0.4g
Cholesterol 52mg
Sodium 163mg
Calcium 42mg
Exchanges:
1 Grain
1 Fat

1. Line 12 muffin cups with paper baking liners. Place 1 wafer in each liner. Place cottage cheese in container of an electric blender. Cover and process until smooth; combine with Neufchâtel in a bowl. Beat at medium speed of an electric mixer until creamy. Mix in sugar. Add rind and next 3 ingredients; beat until smooth. Spoon over wafers.

2. Bake at 350° for 20 minutes or until almost set. (Do not overbake.) Cool on a wire rack. Remove from pans; chill. Spread yogurt over cheesecakes; top with kiwifruit slices. Yield: 12 servings.

Year-Round Recipes

Appetizers and Beverages   77

Breads   89

Desserts   101

Meatless Main Dishes   119

Meats, Poultry, and Seafood   137

Salads and Dressings   167

Side Dishes   185

Soups and Sandwiches   203

Savory Chicken and Peach Salad (page 180)

Delicious, mouthwatering food. Food that you and your family will enjoy. Not only are our year-round recipes good for you, they taste and look better than you'd ever dream.

Imagine enjoying a hearty (and healthy) meal of Steak Diane (page 141), Scalloped Potatoes (page 199), and steamed asparagus, followed by decadent Fruited Crème Brûlée (page 102). Discover those tempting recipes and many others—just flip through these pages. Whether you're preparing a quick breakfast, a last-minute lunch, or a wholesome dinner for family and friends, you'll find the perfect dish for any occasion.

Need something for breakfast on the run? With the batter for Overnight Bran Muffins (page 90) in the refrigerator, you'll have fresh muffins in only 14 minutes.

What about an easy-to-prepare appetizer for a get-together after work? Southwestern Bean Salsa (page 78) takes just 5 minutes to make—and it can chill until you're ready to serve it.

Is it kids' night tonight? If so, Crispy Drumsticks (page 156) and Chili Fries (page 200) will satisfy even the pickiest of eaters.

Unexpected company for dinner? Don't panic. Instead, turn to page 158, and prepare Pesto Pasta and Turkey. It takes just 15 minutes to prepare and 12 minutes to cook, so dinner will be complete before your guests arrive. And if you don't have turkey, you can always use cooked chicken breast instead.

In the mood for a sweet finale to your meal? Serve luscious Lemon Cream Pie (page 109) or rich Honey-Nut Phyllo Slices (page 114) with your favorite gourmet coffee for a satisfying ending to dinner.

Appetizers & Beverages

Fruit Kabobs with Yogurt-Pineapple Dressing (page 79)

Green Chile Dip

Time: Prep 5 minutes; Chill 20 minutes

Per Tablespoon:
Calories 10
Carbohydrate 1.8g
Protein 0.4g
Fat 0.0g
Fiber 0.0g
Cholesterol 0mg
Sodium 95mg
Calcium 13mg
Exchange:
Free

1   (4½-ounce) can chopped green chiles
1   cup nonfat sour cream
1   cup nonfat mayonnaise
¼   cup chopped fresh cilantro
1   teaspoon dried onion flakes
½   teaspoon garlic powder
1   pickled jalapeño pepper, seeded and minced

1. Drain chiles; press between paper towels to remove excess moisture.

2. Combine chiles, sour cream, and remaining ingredients in a medium bowl, stirring well. Cover and chill thoroughly. Serve with fresh raw vegetables or fat-free potato chips. Yield: 2½ cups.

Southwestern Bean Salsa

Time: Prep 5 minutes; Chill 1 hour

Per Tablespoon:
Calories 13
Carbohydrate 2.3g
Protein 0.9g
Fat 0.1g
Fiber 0.3g
Cholesterol 0mg
Sodium 22mg
Calcium 5mg
Exchange:
Free

1   (15-ounce) can black-eyed peas, drained
1   (15-ounce) can red beans, drained
1   cup seeded, chopped tomato
⅔   cup no-salt-added salsa
½   cup thinly sliced green onions
⅓   cup chopped fresh cilantro
3   tablespoons lime juice
½   teaspoon ground cumin
2   cloves garlic, minced
1   jalapeño pepper, seeded and chopped

1. Combine all ingredients in a large bowl, stirring well. Cover and chill at least 1 hour. Serve with no-oil-baked tortilla chips. Yield: 4 cups.

Fruit Kabobs with Yogurt-Pineapple Dip

Time: Prep 17 minutes; Chill 30 minutes

2	medium-size red apples
2	medium pears
2	tablespoons lemon juice
42	unsweetened pineapple chunks
42	seedless red or green grapes (about ½ pound)
42	fresh strawberries, hulled
	Yogurt-Pineapple Dip

1. Cut each apple and pear into 21 bite-size pieces. Combine apple, pear, and lemon juice, tossing gently.

2. Thread apple, pear, pineapple, grapes, and strawberries alternately on 42 (6-inch) skewers. Serve kabobs with Yogurt-Pineapple Dip. Yield 42 appetizers.

Per Appetizer:
Calories 42
Carbohydrate 7.3g
Protein 1.3g
Fat 1.2g
Fiber 1.0g
Cholesterol 4mg
Sodium 38mg
Calcium 31mg
Exchange:
½ Fruit

Yogurt-Pineapple Dip

1	(8-ounce) package reduced-fat cream cheese, softened
2	(8-ounce) cartons vanilla low-fat yogurt
1	teaspoon lemon juice
½	teaspoon grated orange rind
⅛	teaspoon coconut extract
1	(8-ounce) can unsweetened crushed pineapple, drained

1. Beat cream cheese at medium speed of an electric mixer until light and fluffy; add yogurt and next 3 ingredients. Beat until smooth. Stir in pineapple. Cover and chill thoroughly. Yield: 3½ cups.

Sesame Wonton Chips

Time: Prep 7 minutes; Cook 6 minutes

Per Chip:
Calories 7
Carbohydrate 0.7g
Protein 0.4g
Fat 0.3g
Fiber 0.0g
Cholesterol 3mg
Sodium 26mg
Calcium 4mg
Exchange:
Free

1 egg white, lightly beaten
1 tablespoon low-sodium soy sauce
½ teaspoon garlic powder
⅛ teaspoon ground ginger
12 fresh or frozen wonton wrappers, thawed
Vegetable cooking spray
1 tablespoon sesame seeds, toasted

1. Combine first 4 ingredients in a small bowl.

2. Cut each wonton wrapper in half diagonally. Place in a 15- x 10- x 1-inch jellyroll pan coated with cooking spray. Brush egg white mixture over wrappers. Sprinkle evenly with sesame seeds. Bake at 375° for 6 minutes or until crisp and lightly browned. Remove from pan; let cool completely on wire racks. Yield: 2 dozen.

Mushroom Crostini on Greens

Time: Prep 10 minutes

Per Serving:
Calories 135
Carbohydrate 23.4g
Protein 5.5g
Fat 2.8g
Fiber 2.1g
Cholesterol 0mg
Sodium 316mg
Calcium 57mg
Exchanges:
1 Vegetable
1 Grain

Vegetable cooking spray
2 teaspoons olive oil, divided
2 (8-ounce) packages sliced fresh mushrooms
1 tablespoon minced fresh parsley
1½ teaspoons chopped fresh thyme
¼ teaspoon salt
¼ teaspoon freshly ground pepper
1 clove garlic, crushed
1 clove garlic, halved
6 cups mixed baby salad greens
1½ tablespoons lemon juice
6 (½-inch-thick) slices farmers' bread, toasted

1. Coat a large nonstick skillet with cooking spray, and add 1 teaspoon olive oil. Place skillet over medium-high heat until hot. Add mushrooms, and sauté 3 minutes. Add parsley, thyme, salt, freshly ground pepper, and crushed garlic; sauté 5 minutes. Set mushroom mixture aside, and keep warm.

2. Rub inside of a large bowl with cut sides of halved garlic. Add remaining 1 teaspoon oil, greens, and lemon juice to bowl; toss well. Arrange greens on individual salad plates. Top bread slices with mushroom mixture; place over greens. Yield: 6 appetizer servings.

Baked Zucchini Wedges

Time: Prep 9 minutes; Cook 15 minutes

½ cup fine, dry breadcrumbs
3 tablespoons grated Parmesan cheese
½ teaspoon dried Italian seasoning
¼ teaspoon salt
⅛ teaspoon ground red pepper
⅛ teaspoon garlic powder
3 small zucchini
½ cup fat-free egg substitute
3 tablespoons all-purpose flour
Olive oil-flavored vegetable cooking spray

Per Appetizer:
Calories 26
Carbohydrate 3.9g
Protein 1.5g
Fat 0.5g
Fiber 0.3g
Cholesterol 1mg
Sodium 81mg
Calcium 24mg
Exchange:
1 Vegetable

1. Combine first 6 ingredients in a small bowl, and set aside.

2. Cut each zucchini lengthwise into 6 wedges. Dip zucchini wedges in egg substitute, and dredge in flour.

3. Dip wedges in egg substitute again; dredge in breadcrumb mixture. Place wedges in a single layer on a baking sheet coated with cooking spray.

4. Bake at 400° for 15 to 20 minutes or until golden. Serve warm or at room temperature. Yield: 18 appetizers.

Commercial marinara sauce makes an excellent low-fat dip for Baked Zucchini Wedges.

Turkey-Spinach Pinwheels

Time: Prep 6 minutes; Chill 1 hour

½ cup nonfat cream cheese, softened
1 tablespoon pesto
2 teaspoons Dijon mustard
4 (8-inch) fat-free flour tortillas
1 medium tomato, seeded and very thinly sliced
12 (½-ounce) slices fat-free turkey breast
16 large spinach leaves, stems removed

1. Combine first 3 ingredients in a small bowl, stirring well. Spread over 1 side of each tortilla. Arrange tomato slices evenly over cream cheese mixture; top with turkey and spinach leaves.

2. Roll up tortillas, jellyroll fashion. Wrap each roll in plastic wrap, and chill at least 1 hour. Remove plastic wrap, and cut each roll into 8 slices. Yield: 32 appetizers.

Seed the tomato to keep Turkey-Spinach Pinwheels from getting soggy.

Louisiana Crab Cakes

Time: Prep 8 minutes; Cook 12 minutes

1 pound fresh lump crabmeat, drained
1½ cups soft breadcrumbs
3 tablespoons finely chopped green onions
2 tablespoons fresh lemon juice
2 tablespoons nonfat mayonnaise
½ teaspoon paprika
⅛ teaspoon salt
1 egg white, lightly beaten
1 jalapeño pepper, seeded and finely chopped
   Vegetable cooking spray
2 teaspoons vegetable oil, divided
   Lemon wedges (optional)
   Fresh chives (optional)

1. Combine first 9 ingredients in a medium bowl, stirring well. Shape mixture into 8 (½-inch-thick) patties.

2. Coat a large nonstick skillet with cooking spray, and add 1 teaspoon oil. Place over medium heat until hot. Place 4 patties in skillet, and cook 3 minutes on each side or until golden. Repeat procedure with remaining 1 teaspoon oil and 4 patties. If desired, garnish with lemon wedges and chives. Yield: 8 appetizers.

Note: You can serve these crab cakes with fat-free tartar sauce or low-sodium cocktail sauce.

Ginger-Marinated Shrimp and Scallops

Time: Prep 15 minutes; Marinate 1 hour

12	unpeeled large fresh shrimp
4	cups water
4	ounces bay scallops
⅓	cup rice wine vinegar
2	tablespoons finely chopped green onions
1	tablespoon low-sodium soy sauce
½	teaspoon dark sesame oil
¼	teaspoon garlic powder
⅛	teaspoon ground ginger
2	cups shredded fresh spinach

Per Serving:
Calories 109
Carbohydrate 1.4g
Protein 19.2g
Fat 2.1g
Fiber 1.2g
Cholesterol 157mg
Sodium 309mg
Calcium 64mg
Exchanges:
2½ Lean Meat

1. Peel and devein shrimp, leaving tails intact. Bring water to a boil in a saucepan. Add shrimp and scallops; cook 2 minutes or until shrimp turn pink. Drain well, and set aside.

2. Combine vinegar and next 5 ingredients in a heavy-duty, zip-top plastic bag; add shrimp and scallops. Seal bag, and shake until seafood is well coated. Marinate in refrigerator 1 hour, turning bag occasionally.

3. Remove seafood from marinade, reserving marinade. Place ½ cup spinach on each serving plate. Arrange shrimp and scallops evenly on spinach. Drizzle with marinade. Yield: 4 appetizer servings.

Mussels in Tomato-Wine Sauce

Mussels in Tomato-Wine Sauce

Time: Prep 14 minutes; Cook 8 minutes

Per Serving:
Calories 121
Carbohydrate 18.5g
Protein 6.9g
Fat 2.4g
Fiber 1.8g
Cholesterol 9mg
Sodium 196mg
Calcium 80mg
Exchanges:
1 Grain
½ Lean Meat

1	pound fresh mussels
2	teaspoons olive oil
1	cup chopped onion
3	cloves garlic, minced
2	(14½-ounce) cans no-salt-added whole tomatoes, drained and chopped
½	cup dry white wine
⅓	cup chopped fresh basil
¼	teaspoon freshly ground pepper
12	(½-inch-thick) slices French baguette, toasted
	Fresh basil sprigs (optional)

1. Remove beards on mussels, and scrub shells with a brush. Discard open, cracked, or heavy mussels (they're filled with sand). Set aside remaining mussels.

2. Heat oil in a large saucepan over medium-high heat until hot. Add onion and garlic; sauté 4 minutes or until tender. Add tomato and wine; bring to a boil. Add mussels, chopped basil, and pepper. Cover, reduce heat to medium-low, and simmer 3 to 5 minutes or until mussels open. Discard unopened mussels. Spoon mussels mixture into individual serving bowls. Serve with baguette slices. Garnish with basil sprigs, if desired. Yield: 6 appetizer servings.

Black Currant and Raspberry Coolers

Time: Prep 10 minutes; Freeze 1 hour

4½	cups apple-raspberry fruit juice blend, divided
14	fresh raspberries
14	fresh mint leaves
2½	cups water
4	black currant-flavored tea bags

Per Serving:
Calories 72
Carbohydrate 18.4g
Protein 0.1g
Fat 0.0g
Fiber 0.5g
Cholesterol 0mg
Sodium 18mg
Calcium 4mg
Exchange:
1 Fruit

1. Pour 1 cup fruit juice into an ice cube tray; place 1 raspberry and 1 mint leaf in each section of ice cube tray. Freeze until firm.

2. Bring water to a boil in a medium saucepan. Add tea bags; remove from heat. Cover and steep 10 minutes. Remove and discard tea bags.

3. Combine tea and remaining 3½ cups juice in a large pitcher. Cover; chill. Place frozen juice cubes in glasses; pour tea mixture over cubes. Yield: 6 (1-cup) servings.

Black Currant and Raspberry Coolers

Jenny pours herself a glass of refreshing Peach Spritzers.

Peach Spritzers

Per Serving:	Time: Prep 5 minutes
Calories 110	
Carbohydrate 13.6g	1½ cups sweet white wine, chilled
Protein 0.4g	1½ cups peach nectar, chilled
Fat 0.2g	1 cup club soda, chilled
Fiber 0.2g	
Cholesterol 0mg	**1.** Combine all ingredients in a small pitcher, stirring well. Serve
Sodium 26mg	immediately over ice. Yield: 4 (1-cup) servings.
Calcium 14mg	
Exchanges:	**Note:** Wines are now available in small bottles containing
1 Fruit	6 ounces (¾ cup) wine.
1 Fat	

Tangy Cranberry Coolers

Time: Prep 5 minutes

¾ cup cranberry juice cocktail, chilled
½ cup unsweetened apple juice, chilled
2 tablespoons fresh lime juice, chilled
1 tablespoon sugar
1 (6-ounce) can unsweetened pink grapefruit juice, chilled
   Fresh lime slices (optional)

1. Combine first 5 ingredients in a small pitcher, stirring well. Serve over ice. Garnish with lime slices, if desired. Yield: 2 (1-cup) servings.

Per Serving:
Calories 141
Carbohydrate 35.7g
Protein 0.6g
Fat 0.2g
Fiber 0.1g
Cholesterol 0mg
Sodium 6mg
Calcium 14mg
Exchanges:
2½ Fruit

Tangy Cranberry Coolers

Mocha Milk Shakes

Time: Prep 5 minutes; Chill 15 minutes

1 cup hot water
2 teaspoons espresso powder
2 cups vanilla fudge swirl fat-free ice cream
½ cup skim milk
½ cup ice cubes
3 tablespoons chocolate syrup

1. Combine water and espresso powder, stirring well. Cover mixture, and chill.

2. Combine chilled espresso, ice cream, and remaining ingredients in container of an electric blender; cover and process until smooth, stopping once to scrape down sides. Serve immediately. Yield: 4 (1-cup) servings.

Note: You can substitute vanilla fat-free ice cream for vanilla fudge swirl.

Per Serving:
Calories 150
Carbohydrate 32.7g
Protein 4.6g
Fat 0.2g
Fiber 1.0g
Cholesterol 1mg
Sodium 101mg
Calcium 89mg
Exchanges:
2 Grain

Spiced Coffee

Time: Prep 5 minutes

Per Serving:
Calories 9
Carbohydrate 1.3g
Protein 0.2g
Fat 0.0g
Fiber 0.1g
Cholesterol 0mg
Sodium 5mg
Calcium 8mg
Exchange:
Free

¾ cup ground Colombian coffee
¾ teaspoon ground cinnamon
¼ teaspoon ground nutmeg
2 teaspoons vanilla extract
8½ cups water

1. Place coffee in filter basket; sprinkle with cinnamon, nutmeg, and vanilla. Add water to coffeemaker; brew according to manufacturer's directions. Yield: 8 (1-cup) servings.

Warm Citrus Cider

Time: Prep 5 minutes; Cook 15 minutes

Per Serving:
Calories 123
Carbohydrate 30.3g
Protein 0.5g
Fat 0.2g
Fiber 0.5g
Cholesterol 0mg
Sodium 7mg
Calcium 20mg
Exchanges:
2 Fruit

1 teaspoon grated orange rind
¼ teaspoon ground cinnamon
⅛ teaspoon ground allspice
2 whole cloves
1¾ cups unsweetened apple cider
½ cup unsweetened orange juice
2 (3-inch) sticks cinnamon (optional)

1. Place first 4 ingredients on a 4-inch square of cheesecloth or on a coffee filter; tie with string.

2. Pour cider and orange juice into a small saucepan; add spice bag. Cook, uncovered, over low heat 15 minutes, stirring occasionally. Remove and discard spice bag. Pour cider into mugs. Garnish with cinnamon sticks, if desired. Yield: 2 (1-cup) servings.

Breads

Whole Wheat Casserole Bread (page 98)

Overnight Bran Muffins

Time: Prep 10 minutes; Chill 8 hours; Cook 14 minutes

Per Muffin:
Calories 156
Carbohydrate 29.2g
Protein 4.0g
Fat 3.3g
Fiber 1.9g
Cholesterol 19mg
Sodium 288mg
Calcium 31mg
Exchanges:
1½ Grain
½ Fruit
1 Fat

2½   cups all-purpose flour
1½   teaspoons baking soda
1   teaspoon salt
4   cups wheat bran flake cereal with raisins
1   cup mixed dried fruit
⅔   cup sugar
2   eggs, lightly beaten
2   cups nonfat buttermilk
¼   cup corn oil
    Vegetable cooking spray

1. Combine first 6 ingredients in a large bowl; make a well in center of mixture.

2. Combine eggs, buttermilk, and oil. Add buttermilk mixture to dry ingredients, stirring just until moistened. Cover and chill at least 8 hours.

3. Spoon batter into muffin pans coated with cooking spray, filling about three-fourths full. Bake at 400° for 14 to 15 minutes or until muffins are golden. Remove muffins from pans immediately. Yield: 2 dozen.

You can make the batter for Overnight Bran Muffins ahead and store it in the refrigerator up to three days.

Raspberry-Filled Cinnamon Muffins

Time: Prep 10 minutes; Cook 20 minutes

Per Muffin:
Calories 153
Carbohydrate 25.7g
Protein 2.6g
Fat 4.6g
Fiber 0.5g
Cholesterol 18mg
Sodium 116mg
Calcium 63mg
Exchanges:
1½ Grain
1 Fat

1½   cups all-purpose flour
2½   teaspoons baking powder
¼   teaspoon salt
½   cup sugar
1   teaspoon ground cinnamon
1   egg, lightly beaten
⅔   cup low-fat buttermilk
¼   cup margarine, melted
    Vegetable cooking spray
¼   cup seedless raspberry preserves
1   tablespoon sugar
¼   teaspoon ground cinnamon

1. Combine first 5 ingredients in a medium bowl; make a well in center of mixture. Combine egg, buttermilk, and margarine. Add to flour mixture, stirring just until moistened.

2. Spoon about 1 tablespoon batter into each of 12 muffin cups coated with cooking spray. Spoon 1 teaspoon preserves into center of each muffin cup (do not spread over batter), and top with remaining batter.

3. Combine 1 tablespoon sugar and ¼ teaspoon cinnamon; stir well. Sprinkle over muffins. Bake at 400° for 20 minutes or until muffins spring back when touched lightly in center. Remove from pans immediately, and let cool on a wire rack. Yield: 1 dozen.

Raspberry-Filled Cinnamon Muffins

Jenny serves Cranberry-Walnut Scones to grandchildren Sydney, Zachery, and Remington as Picasso (the dog) hovers near.

Cranberry-Walnut Scones

Time: Prep 10 minutes; Cook 15 minutes

Per Scone:
Calories 153
Carbohydrate 26.3g
Protein 3.5g
Fat 3.6g
Fiber 0.9g
Cholesterol 1mg
Sodium 71mg
Calcium 98mg
Exchanges:
1½ Grain
1 Fat

2	cups all-purpose flour
1	tablespoon baking powder
¼	teaspoon baking soda
⅓	cup sugar
2	tablespoons margarine
⅓	cup dried cranberries
1	cup nonfat buttermilk
1	tablespoon vanilla extract
	Vegetable cooking spray
3	tablespoons chopped walnuts
1½	teaspoons sugar

1. Combine first 4 ingredients in a medium bowl; cut in margarine with a pastry blender until mixture resembles coarse meal. Stir in cranberries. Add buttermilk and vanilla, stirring with a fork until dry ingredients are moistened.

2. Spoon 2 heaping tablespoonfuls of dough, 2 inches apart, onto baking sheets coated with cooking spray. Sprinkle evenly with walnuts and 1½ teaspoons sugar. Bake at 400° for 15 to 17 minutes or until golden. Yield: 1 dozen.

Quick French Toast

Time: Prep 6 minutes; Cook 11 minutes

- 4 (1-ounce) Vienna bread slices
   Vegetable cooking spray
- 1 cup skim milk
- ¾ cup fat-free egg substitute
- 1 tablespoon sugar
- ½ teaspoon vanilla extract
   Dash of salt
- 2 teaspoons cinnamon sugar
- 3 tablespoons maple syrup

1. Cut each bread slice diagonally into 4 triangles, and arrange triangles in a nonstick skillet coated with cooking spray. Combine milk and next 4 ingredients; pour over bread.

2. Cover and cook over medium heat 11 minutes or until mixture is set. Remove from heat; sprinkle with cinnamon sugar. Cut into 3 wedges, and drizzle 1 tablespoon syrup over each wedge. Yield: 3 wedges.

Note: You can make your own cinnamon sugar by combining one part ground cinnamon to two parts granulated sugar.

For variety in these scones, you can substitute dried apricots or currants for the cranberries, and pecans or hazelnuts instead of walnuts.

Per Wedge:
Calories 249
Carbohydrate 45.6g
Protein 12.2g
Fat 1.2g
Fiber 0.9g
Cholesterol 3mg
Sodium 403mg
Calcium 154mg
Exchanges:
3 Grain
1 Lean Meat

Rosemary Sweet Bread

Time: Prep 14 minutes; Cook 35 minutes

Per Serving:
Calories 129
Carbohydrate 26.0g
Protein 3.2g
Fat 1.6g
Fiber 0.8g
Cholesterol 28mg
Sodium 99mg
Calcium 54mg
Exchanges:
1½ Grain

Vegetable cooking spray
1½ teaspoons all-purpose flour
1 cup skim milk
½ cup golden raisins
¼ cup unsweetened applesauce
1 tablespoon finely chopped fresh rosemary
2 eggs
⅔ cup sugar
1 tablespoon margarine, melted
2 cups all-purpose flour
1½ teaspoons baking powder
½ teaspoon salt

1. Coat a 9-inch round cakepan with cooking spray; dust pan with 1½ teaspoons flour. Set pan aside.

2. Combine milk and next 3 ingredients in a small saucepan, and bring to a simmer over medium heat. (Do not boil.) Remove from heat; cover and set aside.

3. Beat eggs at medium speed of an electric mixer until foamy. Add sugar and margarine, beating well. Combine 2 cups flour, baking powder, and salt; add to egg mixture, beating until smooth. Add milk mixture; beat until smooth. (Batter will be thin.)

4. Pour batter into prepared pan. Bake at 350° for 35 minutes or until a wooden pick inserted in center comes out clean. Cool in pan on a wire rack 10 minutes. Remove from pan; cool completely on wire rack. Yield: 16 servings.

You'll find that fresh rosemary adds a pleasant, out-of-the-ordinary flavor to this quick bread. I enjoy having a wedge for breakfast or with a cup of tea for an afternoon snack.

Blueberry Loaf Bread

Blueberry Loaf Bread

Time: Prep 10 minutes; Cook 35 minutes

²/₃ cup all-purpose flour
½ teaspoon baking powder
¼ teaspoon baking soda
    Dash of salt
¼ cup sugar
 1 egg white, lightly beaten
¼ cup plus 2 tablespoons plain nonfat yogurt
 2 teaspoons vegetable oil
½ teaspoon vanilla extract
⅓ cup fresh or frozen blueberries, thawed
    Vegetable cooking spray

Per Slice:
Calories 108
Carbohydrate 20.2g
Protein 2.7g
Fat 1.8g
Fiber 0.6g
Cholesterol 0mg
Sodium 79mg
Calcium 46mg
Exchanges:
1 Grain
½ Fruit

1. Combine first 5 ingredients in a medium bowl; make a well in center of mixture. Combine egg white and next 3 ingredients; add to dry ingredients, stirring mixture just until dry ingredients are moistened. Fold in blueberries.

2. Spoon batter into a 6- x 3- x 2-inch loafpan coated with cooking spray. Bake at 350° for 35 to 40 minutes or until a wooden pick inserted in center comes out clean. Remove from pan immediately, and let cool on a wire rack. Yield: 6 (1-inch) slices.

Zucchini-Orange Bread

Time: Prep 10 minutes; Cook 40 minutes

Per Slice:
Calories 93
Carbohydrate 17.2g
Protein 1.9g
Fat 1.9g
Fiber 0.4g
Cholesterol 0mg
Sodium 45mg
Calcium 33mg
Exchange:
1 Grain

1   cup finely shredded zucchini
1¾   cups all-purpose flour
2½   teaspoons baking powder
¼   teaspoon salt
½   cup sugar
1   teaspoon grated orange rind
½   cup unsweetened orange juice
⅓   cup fat-free egg substitute
2   tablespoons vegetable oil
½   teaspoon orange extract
     Vegetable cooking spray

1. Press zucchini between paper towels to remove excess moisture. Combine zucchini, flour, and next 4 ingredients in a large bowl.

2. Combine orange juice and next 3 ingredients, stirring well. Add orange juice mixture to zucchini mixture, stirring just until dry ingredients are moistened.

3. Spoon batter into an 8½- x 4½- x 3-inch loafpan coated with cooking spray. Bake at 375° for 40 to 45 minutes or until a wooden pick inserted in center comes out clean. Let cool in pan 10 minutes; remove from pan, and let cool completely on a wire rack. Yield: 16 (½-inch) slices.

Irish Wheaten Bread

Time: Prep 8 minutes; Cook 45 minutes

Per Wedge:
Calories 184
Carbohydrate 32.7g
Protein 6.3g
Fat 3.5g
Fiber 13g
Cholesterol 1mg
Sodium 337mg
Calcium 46mg
Exchanges:
2 Grain
1 Fat

2   cups all-purpose flour
2   cups whole wheat flour
1   teaspoon baking soda
1   teaspoon salt
2   tablespoons sugar
3   tablespoons chilled stick margarine, cut into small pieces
1⅓ cups low-fat buttermilk
2   egg whites
     Vegetable cooking spray

Irish Wheaten Bread

1. Position knife blade in food processor bowl. Place first 5 ingredients in processor bowl, and pulse until well blended. Drop margarine through food chute with processor running, and process 10 seconds.

2. Combine buttermilk and egg whites; stir well. Pour buttermilk mixture through food chute with processor running, and process 20 seconds or until dough leaves sides of bowl and forms a ball. Turn dough out onto a lightly floured surface, and lightly knead about 10 times.

3. Pat dough into an 8-inch round cakepan coated with cooking spray, and cut a ¼-inch-deep X in top of dough. Bake at 375° for 45 minutes or until lightly browned. Remove bread from pan, and let cool completely on a wire rack. Yield: 12 wedges.

I've found that the secret to tender Irish Wheaten Bread is in your hands: Don't overwork the dough—just lightly knead it. This helps give the bread its unique character. The bread splits around the middle as it bakes, sort of like a large biscuit.

Whole Wheat Casserole Bread

Time: Prep 10 minutes; Rest/Rise 45 minutes; Cook 25 minutes

Per Wedge:
Calories 133
Carbohydrate 25.4g
Protein 4.3g
Fat 2.0g
Fiber 2.5g
Cholesterol 0mg
Sodium 174mg
Calcium 9mg
Exchanges:
1½ Grain

1	package active dry yeast
¾	cup warm water (105° to 115°)
1	cup all-purpose flour, divided
1	cup whole wheat flour
2	tablespoons sugar
2	tablespoons fat-free egg substitute
1½	tablespoons reduced-calorie margarine, melted
½	teaspoon salt
	Vegetable cooking spray

1. Combine yeast and warm water in a 1-cup liquid measuring cup; let stand 5 minutes. Combine yeast mixture, ½ cup all-purpose flour, and next 5 ingredients in a medium bowl, stirring well. Gradually stir in enough of remaining ½ cup all-purpose flour to make a soft dough. (Dough will be sticky.) Let dough rest 15 minutes; shape into a ball.

2. Place dough in a round 1-quart casserole heavily coated with cooking spray. Cover and let rise in a warm place (85°), free from drafts, 30 minutes or until doubled in bulk. Bake at 375° for 25 minutes or until loaf sounds hollow when tapped. (Cover with aluminum foil the last 10 minutes of baking to prevent excessive browning, if necessary.) Remove bread from casserole immediately, and let cool on a wire rack. Yield: 8 wedges.

Cheesy Garlic Bread

Time: Prep 5 minutes; Cook 20 minutes

1	(1-pound) loaf Italian bread
	Butter-flavored vegetable cooking spray
¼	cup freshly grated Parmesan cheese
1	tablespoon minced fresh parsley
¼	teaspoon garlic powder

1. Slice bread in half lengthwise; coat cut surface of each half with cooking spray. Combine cheese, parsley, and garlic powder; sprinkle over cut surface of one half of bread. Top with other half of bread.

2. Wrap bread in aluminum foil; bake at 350° for 20 minutes or until thoroughly heated. Yield: 20 (½-inch) slices.

Per Slice:
Calories 69
Carbohydrate 12.9g
Protein 2.6g
Fat 0.6g
Fiber 0.6g
Cholesterol 1mg
Sodium 156mg
Calcium 21mg
Exchange:
1 Grain

Herbed Breadsticks

Time: Prep 5 minutes; Cook 25 minutes

1	(8-ounce) loaf French bread
1	tablespoon olive oil
1	clove garlic, halved
¾	teaspoon dried oregano
¾	teaspoon dried basil
⅛	teaspoon salt

1. Cut bread in half crosswise, and cut each piece in half horizontally. Brush oil evenly over cut sides of bread; rub with cut sides of garlic. Sprinkle oregano, basil, and salt over bread. Cut each piece of bread lengthwise into 3 sticks. Place breadsticks on a baking sheet; bake at 300° for 25 minutes or until crisp. Serve warm. Yield: 1 dozen.

Per Breadstick:
Calories 75
Carbohydrate 12.4g
Protein 2.1g
Fat 1.8g
Fiber 0.4g
Cholesterol 1mg
Sodium 152mg
Calcium 13mg
Exchange:
1 Grain

Cinnamon Crisps

Cinnamon Crisps

Time: Prep 5 minutes; Cook 12 minutes

Per Serving:
Calories 123
Carbohydrate 21.9g
Protein 2.6g
Fat 2.6g
Fiber 1.1g
Cholesterol 0mg
Sodium 144mg
Calcium 45mg
Exchanges:
1½ Grain
1 Fat

1 tablespoon hot water
½ teaspoon vanilla extract
1½ tablespoons sugar
1 teaspoon ground cinnamon
4 (6-inch) flour tortillas
   Vegetable cooking spray

1. Combine water and vanilla in a small bowl. Combine sugar and cinnamon; stir well. Lightly coat both sides of 2 tortillas with cooking spray; lightly brush each side with water mixture, and sprinkle each side with sugar mixture.

2. Place coated tortillas on a wire rack in a 15- x 10- x 1-inch jellyroll pan. Bake at 400° for 6 minutes or until lightly browned. Repeat procedure with remaining 2 tortillas and sugar mixture. Yield: 4 servings.

I've found that it's easiest to combine the sugar and cinnamon in an empty saltshaker. Then I can sprinkle the mixture over the tortillas for an even coating.

Desserts

Fresh Strawberry Sauce (page 102)

Fresh Strawberry Sauce

Time: Prep 3 minutes; Stand 1 hour; Cook 5 minutes;
Chill 30 minutes

Per Tablespoon:
Calories 8
Carbohydrate 2.1g
Protein 0.1g
Fat 0.0g
Fiber 0.0g
Cholesterol 0mg
Sodium 0mg
Calcium 2mg
Exchange:
Free

4   cups fresh strawberries, sliced
¼   cup sugar
1   tablespoon cornstarch
½   teaspoon almond extract
    Frozen reduced-calorie whipped topping,
        thawed (optional)

1. Combine strawberries and sugar in a small bowl. Let stand until syrup forms (about 1 hour). Drain syrup into a 2-cup glass measure, reserving strawberries. Add enough water to syrup to make 1½ cups.

2. Combine syrup mixture and cornstarch in a small saucepan; stir well. Cook over medium heat, stirring constantly, until smooth and thick. Cover and chill at least 30 minutes.

3. Stir in reserved strawberries and almond extract before serving. Serve sauce over commercial shortcakes, fat-free pound cake, or nonfat ice cream. Garnish each serving with whipped topping, if desired. Yield: 3 cups.

Fruited Crème Brûlée

Time: Prep 14 minutes; Cook 2 minutes

Per Serving:
Calories 123
Carbohydrate 21.4g
Protein 2.1g
Fat 4.0g
Fiber 2.9g
Cholesterol 11mg
Sodium 46mg
Calcium 41mg
Exchanges:
1½ Fruit
1 Fat

2   cups fresh pineapple chunks
2   cups fresh strawberries, halved
2   medium kiwifruit, peeled and sliced
¼   cup low-fat sour cream
2   ounces Neufchâtel cheese, softened
⅓   cup firmly packed brown sugar

1. Combine first 3 ingredients in a large bowl, and stir gently. Spoon fruit mixture evenly into six 6-ounce ovenproof ramekins or custard cups.

2. Combine sour cream and Neufchâtel cheese, stirring well; spoon over fruit mixture.

3. Place ramekins on a baking sheet, and sprinkle evenly with brown sugar. Broil 5½ inches from heat (with electric oven door partially opened) 2 minutes or until sugar melts. Serve immediately. Yield: 6 servings.

Tropical Fruit in Custard Sauce

Time: Prep 19 minutes; Chill 1 hour

1	(10½-ounce) loaf commercial angel food cake
¼	cup sugar
3	tablespoons cornstarch
¼	teaspoon salt
1¾	cups skim milk
2	tablespoons fat-free egg substitute
3	tablespoons cream sherry
1	(8-ounce) can pineapple chunks in juice, drained
½	cup sliced fresh strawberries
1	medium mango, peeled, seeded, and cubed
1	kiwifruit, peeled and sliced
1	carambola (star fruit), sliced
	Fresh mint sprigs (optional)

Per Serving:
Calories 218
Carbohydrate 47.5g
Protein 5.1g
Fat 0.5g
Fiber 1.7g
Cholesterol 1mg
Sodium 187mg
Calcium 127mg
Exchanges:
2 Grain
1 Fruit

1. Cut cake into 1-inch cubes; set aside. Combine sugar, cornstarch, and salt in a saucepan; gradually stir in milk. Cook over medium heat, stirring constantly, until mixture comes to a boil. Cook, stirring constantly, 1 minute. Remove from heat.

2. Gradually stir one-fourth of hot milk mixture into egg substitute. Place remaining hot milk mixture over low heat; stir in egg substitute mixture. Cook, stirring constantly, 1 minute or until mixture is thickened. Remove from heat. Cool slightly, and add cream sherry, stirring well. Cover and chill thoroughly.

3. Combine custard mixture, cake cubes, pineapple chunks, and next 4 ingredients in a bowl; toss gently. Cover and chill thoroughly.

4. To serve, spoon custard sauce evenly into individual dessert bowls. Garnish with mint sprigs, if desired. Yield: 6 servings.

Poached Pears with Raspberry Sherbet

Time: Prep 10 minutes; Cook 15 minutes; Chill 1 hour

Per Serving:
Calories 133
Carbohydrate 29.9g
Protein 1.1g
Fat 2.3g
Fiber 2.2g
Cholesterol 0mg
Sodium 34mg
Calcium 31mg
Exchanges:
1 Grain
1 Fruit

3 large ripe pears
2 teaspoons lemon juice
1 cup white Zinfandel or other blush wine
½ cup sugar
½ cup unsweetened apple juice
1 tablespoon lemon juice
1 (1-ounce) square semisweet chocolate, melted
1½ cups raspberry sherbet
Fresh raspberries (optional)
Fresh mint sprigs (optional)

Poached Pears with Raspberry Sherbet

1. Peel and core pears; cut in half lengthwise, and brush with 2 teaspoons lemon juice.

2. Combine wine and next 3 ingredients in a large saucepan; bring to a boil. Add pears; cover, reduce heat, and simmer 15 minutes or until tender, turning once. Transfer pears and poaching liquid to a bowl; cover and chill at least 1 hour.

3. Drizzle half of melted chocolate evenly onto six dessert plates. Transfer pears, cut sides up, to plates, using a slotted spoon. Discard poaching liquid. Top each pear with ¼ cup sherbet. Drizzle with remaining chocolate. If desired, garnish with raspberries and mint sprigs. Serve immediately. Yield: 6 servings.

Double-Chocolate Cupcakes

Time: Prep 21 minutes; Cook 20 minutes

1   (18.25-ounce) package light, 94%-fat-free devil's food
    cake mix
1   cup water
3   eggs
    Vegetable cooking spray
¼   cup semisweet chocolate morsels
¼   cup skim milk
3   tablespoons unsweetened cocoa
2   cups sifted powdered sugar
2   teaspoons vanilla extract
2   tablespoons powdered sugar

Per Cupcake:
Calories 155
Carbohydrate 30.2g
Protein 2.1g
Fat 2.9g
Fiber 0.0g
Cholesterol 27mg
Sodium 175mg
Calcium 28mg
Exchanges:
2 Grain

1. Combine first 3 ingredients in a bowl; beat at medium speed of an electric mixer 2 minutes. Spoon batter evenly into 24 muffin cups coated with cooking spray. Bake at 350° for 20 minutes or until a wooden pick inserted in center comes out clean. Cool in pans on wire racks 10 minutes; remove from pans, and let cool on wire racks.

2. Split each cupcake in half horizontally, using a serrated knife; set aside.

3. Combine chocolate morsels, milk, and cocoa in top of a double boiler; bring water to a boil. Reduce heat to low; cook until chocolate morsels melt, stirring occasionally. Remove from heat; stir in 2 cups powdered sugar and vanilla. Spread bottom half of each cupcake with 2 teaspoons chocolate mixture; place top half of cupcake on chocolate mixture. Sift 2 tablespoons powdered sugar over cupcakes. Yield: 2 dozen.

Angel Food Cake with Caramel-Coffee Sauce

Angel Food Cake with Caramel-Coffee Sauce

Time: Prep 10 minutes

Per Serving:
Calories 184
Carbohydrate 41.3g
Protein 4.6g
Fat 0.2g
Fiber 0.0g
Cholesterol 1mg
Sodium 105mg
Calcium 108mg
Exchanges:
2 ½ Grain

3   tablespoons brown sugar
1   tablespoon cornstarch
½   teaspoon instant espresso powder
1   cup skim milk
½   teaspoon vanilla extract
6   (2-ounce) slices angel food cake

1. Combine first 3 ingredients in a small saucepan, stirring well. Gradually stir in milk; bring to a boil, stirring constantly. Remove from heat; stir in vanilla. Place cake slices on individual dessert plates. Top each serving with 2 tablespoons sauce. Serve immediately. Yield: 6 servings.

Pumpkin-Pecan Pound Cake

Time: Prep 12 minutes; Cook 1 hour and 35 minutes

¾ cup margarine, softened
1½ cups firmly packed brown sugar
1 cup sugar
1¼ cups fat-free egg substitute
1 (16-ounce) can pumpkin
⅓ cup bourbon or orange juice
3 cups all-purpose flour
2 teaspoons baking powder
½ teaspoon baking soda
¼ teaspoon salt
2 teaspoons pumpkin pie spice
¼ cup chopped pecans
Vegetable cooking spray

Per Serving:
Calories 213
Carbohydrate 35.7g
Protein 3.2g
Fat 6.7g
Fiber 1.3g
Cholesterol 0mg
Sodium 143mg
Calcium 49mg
Exchanges:
2 Grain
1 Fat

1. Beat margarine at medium speed of an electric mixer until creamy; gradually add sugars, beating well. Add egg substitute, and beat well.

2. Combine pumpkin and bourbon, stirring well. Combine flour and next 4 ingredients; add to margarine mixture alternately with pumpkin mixture, beginning and ending with flour mixture. Mix well after each addition.

3. Sprinkle pecans over bottom of a 10-inch tube pan coated with cooking spray. Spoon batter over pecans. Bake at 325° for 1 hour and 35 minutes or until a wooden pick inserted in center comes out clean. Cool in pan 10 minutes. Remove cake from pan, and cool completely on a wire rack. Yield: 24 servings.

Orange-Blueberry Streusel Cake

Time: Prep 9 minutes; Cook 25 minutes

Per Serving:
Calories 129
Carbohydrate 27.0g
Protein 1.5g
Fat 2.0g
Fiber 0.1g
Cholesterol 0mg
Sodium 156mg
Calcium 4mg
Exchanges:
1½ Grain

¼ cup sugar
2 tablespoons all-purpose flour
2 teaspoons grated orange rind
½ teaspoon ground cinnamon
1 tablespoon margarine
1 (16.5-ounce) package light, 97%-fat-free wild blueberry muffin mix
¾ cup fresh orange juice
1 teaspoon vanilla extract
1 egg white
Vegetable cooking spray

1. Combine first 4 ingredients; cut in margarine with a pastry blender or two knives until mixture resembles coarse meal. Set aside.

2. Remove blueberries from muffin mix package. Drain and rinse blueberries, and set aside.

3. Combine muffin mix, orange juice, vanilla, and egg white, stirring just until dry ingredients are moistened. Gently fold in blueberries. Pour batter into an 8-inch square baking dish coated with cooking spray. Sprinkle sugar mixture over batter.

4. Bake at 400° for 25 minutes or until a wooden pick inserted in center comes out clean. Let cool in pan on a wire rack. Yield: 12 servings.

Lemon Cream Pie

Time: Prep 11 minutes; Cook 16 minutes; Chill 2 hours

   1   cup low-fat cinnamon graham cracker crumbs (about 7 crackers)
 ¼   cup reduced-calorie margarine, melted
 ¾   cup sugar
 ¼   cup plus 3 tablespoons cornstarch
 ⅛   teaspoon salt
   1   cup water
 ⅔   cup nonfat buttermilk
 ½   cup fat-free egg substitute
   2   teaspoons grated lemon rind
 ½   cup fresh lemon juice
2½   cups frozen reduced-calorie whipped topping, thawed
       Lemon zest (optional)
       Lemon rind curls (optional)
       Fresh mint sprigs (optional)

Per Serving:
Calories 251
Carbohydrate 46.4g
Protein 4.1g
Fat 7.2g
Fiber 0.6g
Cholesterol 1mg
Sodium 175mg
Calcium 47mg
Exchanges:
2 Grain
1 Fruit
1 Fat

1. Combine cracker crumbs and margarine; stir well. Press into bottom and up sides of a 9-inch pieplate. Bake at 350° for 8 to 10 minutes or until golden. Remove from oven; let cool on a wire rack.

2. Combine sugar, cornstarch, and salt in a saucepan; gradually stir in water and buttermilk. Cook over medium heat, stirring constantly, until mixture comes to a boil. Cook 1 minute.

3. Gradually stir about one-fourth of hot mixture into egg substitute; add egg substitute mixture to remaining hot mixture, stirring constantly. Cook over medium heat, stirring constantly, 2 minutes or until thickened. Remove from heat; stir in 2 teaspoons lemon rind and lemon juice.

4. Spoon lemon mixture into prepared crust. Cover; chill at least 2 hours. Spread whipped topping over filling just before serving. If desired, garnish with lemon zest, lemon rind curls, and fresh mint sprigs. Yield: 8 servings.

Lemon Cream Pie

Strawberry Crunch Parfaits

Time: Prep 12 minutes; Cook 20 minutes

Per Serving:
Calories 245
Carbohydrate 40.7g
Protein 6.5g
Fat 7.2g
Fiber 2.9g
Cholesterol 0mg
Sodium 94mg
Calcium 148mg
Exchanges:
2 Grain
½ Fruit
1 Fat

1¼ cups regular oats, uncooked
⅓ cup chopped pecans
2 tablespoons brown sugar
    Vegetable cooking spray
3 tablespoons honey
2 tablespoons margarine, melted
2 teaspoons vanilla extract
1 teaspoon ground cinnamon
4 cups vanilla nonfat frozen yogurt
2 cups sliced fresh strawberries
    Fresh mint sprigs (optional)

1. Combine first 3 ingredients; place in a 13- x 9- x 2-inch pan coated with cooking spray. Combine honey and next 3 ingredients, stirring well; drizzle over oat mixture. Stir well. Bake at 350° for 20 minutes or until golden, stirring occasionally. Spoon oat mixture onto aluminum foil; let cool.

2. Spoon ¼ cup frozen yogurt into each of eight 8-ounce parfait glasses. Top each serving with 2 tablespoons strawberries and 2 tablespoons oat mixture; repeat layers with remaining yogurt, strawberries, and oat mixture. Garnish with mint sprigs, if desired. Yield: 8 servings.

The oat mixture in Strawberry Crunch Parfaits also tastes delicious stirred into vanilla low-fat yogurt or mixed into hot cooked cereal.

Spumoni Loaf

Spumoni Loaf

Time: Prep 10 minutes; Freeze 5 hours

2½ cups lime sherbet, softened
3 tablespoons chopped pistachios, divided
1 (8-ounce) can unsweetened crushed pineapple, drained
1½ cups vanilla low-fat ice cream, softened
2 cups raspberry sherbet, softened

Per Serving:
Calories 173
Carbohydrate 34.3g
Protein 2.7g
Fat 3.5g
Fiber 0.5g
Cholesterol 3mg
Sodium 97mg
Calcium 81mg
Exchanges:
1½ Grain
½ Fruit
1 Fat

1. Line an 8½- x 4½- x 3-inch loafpan with wax paper. Combine lime sherbet and 1½ tablespoons pistachios, stirring well. Spread in bottom of prepared pan; freeze 30 minutes.

2. Press pineapple between paper towels to remove excess moisture. Combine pineapple and ice cream, stirring well. Spread over sherbet mixture; freeze 30 minutes. Spread raspberry sherbet over ice cream mixture. Cover and freeze 4 hours or until firm.

3. Invert spumoni onto a serving platter. Remove wax paper. Top with remaining 1½ tablespoons pistachios. Let stand at room temperature 5 minutes before slicing. Yield: 8 servings.

Refreshing Lemon Sherbet

Refreshing Lemon Sherbet

Time: Prep 10 minutes; Freeze 17 minutes; Ripen 1 hour

Per Serving:
Calories 108
Carbohydrate 23.4g
Protein 2.4g
Fat 1.3g
Fiber 0.0g
Cholesterol 5mg
Sodium 60mg
Calcium 81mg
Exchanges:
1½ Fruit

1   lemon
1   cup sugar
3   cups 2% low-fat milk
½   cup fresh lemon juice
½   cup water
⅛   teaspoon salt

1. Using a vegetable peeler, carefully remove rind from lemon. Position knife blade in a food processor bowl, and add rind and sugar; process until rind is minced. Spoon sugar mixture into a bowl. Add milk and remaining 3 ingredients; stir well.

2. Pour mixture into freezer can of a 2-quart or 1-gallon hand-turned or electric freezer, and freeze according to manufacturer's instructions. Let ripen at least 1 hour. Serve in lemon cups, if desired. Yield: 11 (½-cup) servings.

When removing the lemon rind, be careful not to remove any of the white pith underneath, or your sherbet will taste bitter.

Banana-Chocolate Chip Pops

Time: Prep 5 minutes; Freeze 4 hours

1   cup 1% low-fat chocolate milk
2   small bananas, peeled and cut into chunks
1   (8-ounce) carton coffee-flavored low-fat yogurt
3   tablespoons semisweet chocolate mini-morsels
8   (3-ounce) paper cups
8   wooden sticks

Per Pop:
Calories 108
Carbohydrate 18.0g
Protein 3.3g
Fat 3.2g
Fiber 0.9g
Cholesterol 1mg
Sodium 50mg
Calcium 88mg
Exchanges:
1 Grain
1 Fat

1. Combine first 3 ingredients in container of an electric blender or food processor; cover and process until smooth.

2. Stir in chocolate morsels. Pour mixture evenly into paper cups. Cover tops of cups with aluminum foil, and insert a stick through foil into center of each cup. Freeze at least 4 hours. To serve, remove foil, and peel paper cup away from each pop. Yield: 8 pops.

Banana-Chocolate Chip Pops

Quick Peach Crisps

Time: Prep 5 minutes; Cook 20 minutes

Per Serving:
Calories 143
Carbohydrate 34.0g
Protein 1.9g
Fat 0.9g
Fiber 1.0g
Cholesterol 0mg
Sodium 23mg
Calcium 17mg
Exchanges:
½ Grain
1½ Fruit

1 (16-ounce) can sliced peaches in juice, drained
2 tablespoons sugar
1 teaspoon cornstarch
  Vegetable cooking spray
¼ cup low-fat granola without raisins

1. Combine first 3 ingredients; spoon mixture into two 10-ounce custard cups coated with cooking spray. Place custard cups on a baking sheet, and top with granola. Bake, uncovered, at 400° for 20 minutes or until thoroughly heated and topping is crisp. Yield: 2 servings.

Honey-Nut Phyllo Slices

Time: Prep 17 minutes; Cook 30 minutes

Per Slice:
Calories 101
Carbohydrate 16.6g
Protein 1.6g
Fat 3.6g
Fiber 0.1g
Cholesterol 0mg
Sodium 88mg
Calcium 4mg
Exchanges:
1 Grain
1 Fat

¼ cup honey, divided
1½ tablespoons reduced-calorie margarine
¼ teaspoon ground allspice
  Dash of ground cloves
¼ teaspoon vanilla extract
6 sheets frozen phyllo pastry, thawed
  Butter-flavored vegetable cooking spray
2 tablespoons ground walnuts

1. Combine 3 tablespoons honey and next 3 ingredients in a saucepan; cook over low heat until margarine melts. Remove from heat; stir in vanilla.

2. Cut phyllo in half crosswise. Place 1 sheet phyllo on wax paper (keeping remaining phyllo covered). Lightly coat phyllo with cooking spray. Top with a second sheet of phyllo; coat with cooking spray. Brush with 2 teaspoons honey mixture. Repeat layers twice.

3. Sprinkle top phyllo layer with 1 tablespoon walnuts, leaving a 1-inch margin on long sides. Roll up, jellyroll fashion, starting with long side. Place, seam side down, on a baking sheet coated with cooking spray. Repeat with remaining phyllo, honey mixture, and walnuts.

4. Brush honey mixture over phyllo. Cut each roll diagonally into 4 slices. Bake at 300° for 30 minutes. Drizzle remaining 1 tablespoon honey over warm phyllo. Let cool. Yield: 8 slices.

Molasses Crinkles

Time: Prep 20 minutes; Chill 1 hour; Cook 8 minutes

¼ cup margarine, softened
¾ cup plus 1½ tablespoons sugar, divided
¼ cup molasses
1 egg
2 cups all-purpose flour
2 teaspoons baking soda
¼ teaspoon salt
1¾ teaspoons ground cinnamon, divided
　Vegetable cooking spray

Per Cookie:
Calories 48
Carbohydrate 8.7g
Protein 0.7g
Fat 1.1g
Fiber 0.2g
Cholesterol 5mg
Sodium 78mg
Calcium 6mg
Exchange:
½ Grain

1. Beat margarine at medium speed of an electric mixer until creamy; gradually add ¾ cup sugar, beating well. Add molasses and egg; beat well.

2. Combine flour, baking soda, salt, and 1½ teaspoons cinnamon, stirring well. Gradually add flour mixture to margarine mixture, beating until blended. Cover and chill 1 hour.

3. Combine remaining 1½ table-spoons sugar and ¼ teaspoon cinnamon. Shape dough into 48 (1-inch) balls; roll balls in sugar mixture. Place, 2 inches apart, on cookie sheets coated with cooking spray. Bake at 350° for 8 minutes or until golden. Cool slightly on cookie sheets. Remove from cookie sheets; cool completely on wire racks. Yield: 4 dozen.

Grandsons Brandon and Collin (in Sid's arms) enjoy Molasses Crinkles.

Chocolate Chip-Strawberry Thumbprint Cookies

Chocolate Chip-Strawberry Thumbprint Cookies

Time: Prep 6 minutes; Cook 10 minutes

Per Cookie:
Calories 54
Carbohydrate 8.8g
Protein 0.6g
Fat 1.8g
Fiber 0.2g
Cholesterol 0mg
Sodium 28mg
Calcium 1mg
Exchange:
½ Grain

1 (17.5-ounce) package regular chocolate chip cookie mix
1 cup regular oats, uncooked
⅓ cup water
1 teaspoon vanilla extract
1 egg white
   Vegetable cooking spray
¼ cup plus 2 teaspoons strawberry jam

1. Combine first 5 ingredients; drop by 2 level teaspoonfuls 1 inch apart onto cookie sheets coated with cooking spray.

2. Press center of each cookie with thumb, making an indentation; fill with ¼ teaspoon jam. Bake at 375° for 10 minutes or until golden. Yield: 4½ dozen.

Butterscotch Bars

Time: Prep 12 minutes; Cool 1 hour

    3   tablespoons margarine
    ½   cup firmly packed brown sugar
    2   cups miniature marshmallows
    4   cups oven-toasted crisp rice cereal
    2   cups whole wheat flake cereal
        Vegetable cooking spray

1. Melt margarine in a large saucepan over medium heat. Add sugar; stir well. Add marshmallows; cook, stirring constantly, until marshmallows melt. Remove from heat; stir in cereals.

2. Press cereal mixture evenly into the bottom of a 13- x 9- x 2-inch baking pan coated with cooking spray. Let cool for 1 hour. Cut into 3- x 2-inch bars. Yield: 1½ dozen.

Per Bar:
Calories 92
Carbohydrate 18.0g
Protein 0.8g
Fat 2.0g
Fiber 0.3g
Cholesterol 0mg
Sodium 111mg
Calcium 10mg
Exchange:
1 Grain

Chewy Coffee Brownies

Time: Prep 15 minutes; Cook 18 minutes

Per Brownie:
Calories 129
Carbohydrate 23.0g
Protein 1.8g
Fat 3.5g
Fiber 0.3g
Cholesterol 9mg
Sodium 72mg
Calcium 32mg
Exchanges:
1½ Grain

1½ cups firmly packed dark brown sugar
½ cup reduced-calorie stick margarine
2½ tablespoons instant coffee granules
1 tablespoon vanilla extract
2 egg whites
1 egg
2 cups all-purpose flour
2 teaspoons baking powder
⅛ teaspoon salt
½ cup semisweet chocolate morsels
Vegetable cooking spray

1. Combine first 3 ingredients in a small saucepan. Cook over low heat 4 minutes or until margarine melts and mixture is smooth, stirring often.

2. Combine sugar mixture, vanilla, egg whites, and egg; beat at low speed of an electric mixer until smooth.

3. Combine flour, baking powder, and salt; gradually add to sugar mixture, beating well. Stir in chocolate morsels. Spread batter into a 13- x 9- x 2-inch baking pan coated with cooking spray. Bake at 350° for 18 minutes; let cool in pan. Yield: 2 dozen.

Meatless Main Dishes

Garden Orecchiette (page 134)

West Coast Breakfast Burritos

Time: Prep 5 minutes; Cook 10 minutes

Per Burrito:
Calories 242
Carbohydrate 26.1g
Protein 15.9g
Fat 8.0g
Fiber 2.2g
Cholesterol 9mg
Sodium 418mg
Calcium 183mg
Exchanges:
1 Grain
1 ½ Lean Meat
2 Vegetable
1 Fat

½ cup seeded, chopped tomato
1 tablespoon chopped green onions
1 tablespoon cold water
1 teaspoon seeded, chopped jalapeño pepper
2 teaspoons lime juice
⅛ teaspoon dried oregano
Vegetable cooking spray
½ cup fat-free egg substitute
¼ cup diced ripe avocado
¼ cup nonfat sour cream
2 tablespoons canned chopped green chiles
¼ cup (1 ounce) shredded reduced-fat Monterey Jack cheese
2 (10-inch) flour tortillas, heated

1. Combine first 6 ingredients in a small bowl; set aside.

2. Coat a small nonstick skillet with cooking spray; place over medium heat until hot. Pour egg substitute into skillet. As mixture begins to cook, gently lift edges of omelet with a spatula, and tilt pan to allow uncooked portion to flow underneath. When set, add avocado and next 3 ingredients; stir gently until cheese melts.

3. Spoon egg substitute mixture down center of each tortilla. Roll up tortillas, folding in sides. Place, seam sides down, on serving plates. Top evenly with tomato mixture. Yield: 2 burritos.

Vegetable Frittata

Time: Prep 5 minutes; Cook 15 minutes

Olive oil-flavored vegetable cooking spray
1 tablespoon sliced green onions
2 cloves garlic, minced
1 cup sliced fresh mushrooms
½ cup diced sweet red pepper
¼ cup chopped fresh broccoli flowerets
1½ cups fat-free egg substitute
2 tablespoons grated Parmesan cheese
½ teaspoon dried basil
¼ teaspoon dried oregano
¼ teaspoon pepper
¼ teaspoon salt
⅛ teaspoon dried crushed red pepper
3 tablespoons crumbled feta cheese

Per Serving:
Calories 89
Carbohydrate 4.9g
Protein 11.9g
Fat 2.4g
Fiber 0.9g
Cholesterol 7mg
Sodium 401mg
Calcium 113mg
Exchanges:
1 Lean Meat
1 Vegetable

1. Coat a nonstick skillet with cooking spray; place over medium-high heat until hot. Add onions and garlic; sauté 2 minutes. Add mushrooms, sweet red pepper, and broccoli, sauté 3 additional minutes.

2. Combine egg substitute and next 6 ingredients in a small bowl, stirring well; pour over vegetable mixture. Cover; cook over medium heat 10 minutes or until egg substitute mixture is set. Sprinkle with feta cheese, and serve immediately. Yield: 4 servings.

Sunshine Scramble

Time: Prep 3 minutes; Cook 5 minutes

Per Serving:
Calories 48
Carbohydrate 3.0g
Protein 7.6g
Fat 0.2g
Fiber 0.1g
Cholesterol 0mg
Sodium 255mg
Calcium 41mg
Exchange:
1 Lean Meat

1   cup fat-free egg substitute
¼   cup skim milk
¼   cup nonfat sour cream
¼   teaspoon salt
⅛   teaspoon pepper
¼   cup chopped green onions
     Vegetable cooking spray

1. Combine first 5 ingredients in container of an electric blender or food processor; cover and process 10 seconds or until frothy. Transfer to a medium bowl; stir in green onions.

2. Coat a large nonstick skillet with cooking spray, and place skillet over medium heat until hot. Add egg substitute mixture, and cook until mixture is firm but still moist, stirring often. Yield: 4 servings.

Herbed Gazpacho Omelet

Time: Prep 12 minutes; Cook 18 minutes

Per Serving:
Calories 138
Carbohydrate 11.6g
Protein 9.7g
Fat 5.8g
Fiber 1.1g
Cholesterol 218mg
Sodium 393mg
Calcium 51mg
Exchanges:
2 Vegetable
1 Medium-Fat Meat

     Vegetable cooking spray
2   tablespoons minced onion
2   cloves garlic, minced
2   egg yolks
1   tablespoon skim milk
3   egg whites
1   tablespoon all-purpose flour
½   teaspoon sugar
¼   teaspoon salt
⅛   teaspoon pepper
¼   cup seeded, chopped cucumber
2   tablespoons diced green pepper
3   tablespoons no-salt-added tomato sauce
2   teaspoons minced fresh basil
4   (¼-inch-thick) tomato slices
¼   cup alfalfa sprouts
     Cucumber slices (optional)
     Basil sprigs (optional)

Herbed Gazpacho Omelet

Step 2: *Beat egg yolks until thick and pale.*

Step 3: *Beat egg whites until soft peaks form.*

Step 3: *Fold egg white mixture into egg yolk mixture.*

Step 5: *Loosen omelet, and fold in half.*

1. Coat a nonstick skillet with cooking spray, and place over medium-high heat until hot. Add onion and garlic; sauté until tender. Remove from skillet; set aside.

2. Beat egg yolks at high speed of an electric mixer until thick and pale. Add milk, and beat until well blended; set aside.

3. Beat egg whites until soft peaks form. Add flour and next 3 ingredients; beat until stiff peaks form. Fold egg white mixture into egg yolk mixture.

4. Coat skillet with cooking spray, and place over medium heat until hot. Spread egg mixture evenly in skillet; top with onion mixture. Cover, reduce heat to medium-low, and cook 15 minutes or until center is set.

5. Combine chopped cucumber and next 3 ingredients; stir well. Arrange tomato over half of omelet. Spread cucumber mixture over tomato; top with alfalfa sprouts. Loosen omelet with a spatula; fold in half. Slide onto a warm plate; cut in half. Garnish with cucumber slices and basil, if desired. Serve immediately. Yield: 2 servings.

Artichoke-Cheddar Strata

Time: Prep 8 minutes; Chill 3 hours; Stand 30 minutes; Cook 1 hour

Per Serving:
Calories 179
Carbohydrate 21.4g
Protein 15.0g
Fat 4.3g
Fiber 0.5g
Cholesterol 12mg
Sodium 445mg
Calcium 335mg
Exchanges:
½ Grain
1 Vegetable
1½ Lean Meat
½ Skim Milk

Vegetable cooking spray
1 teaspoon margarine
½ cup chopped green onions
3 slices whole wheat bread, cubed
¾ cup (3 ounces) shredded reduced-fat Cheddar cheese
1 (14-ounce) can artichoke hearts, drained and quartered
1 (4-ounce) jar sliced pimiento, drained
¾ cup fat-free egg substitute
½ teaspoon dry mustard
⅛ teaspoon ground red pepper
1 (12-ounce) can evaporated skimmed milk

1. Coat a small nonstick skillet with cooking spray; add margarine. Place over medium heat until margarine melts. Add green onions; sauté 3 to 4 minutes or until tender. Remove from heat, and set aside.

2. Arrange half of bread cubes in a 9-inch quiche dish coated with cooking spray. Top with half of cheese, half of artichoke hearts, half of green onions, and half of pimiento. Repeat layers with remaining bread cubes, cheese, artichoke, green onions, and pimiento.

3. Combine egg substitute and remaining 3 ingredients; stir well. Pour over mixture in quiche dish. Cover and chill at least 3 hours or overnight.

4. Let stand at room temperature 30 minutes. Bake, uncovered, at 350° for 1 hour or until set. Yield: 6 servings.

Mexican Vegetable Pies

Time: Prep 15 minutes; Cook 14 minutes

Vegetable cooking spray
1½ cups sliced green onions
½ cup chopped green pepper
2 cloves garlic, minced
1½ cups frozen whole-kernel corn, thawed
½ cup chunky picante sauce
2 tablespoons minced fresh cilantro
2 tablespoons lime juice
2 (16-ounce) cans pinto beans, drained
2 medium tomatoes, chopped
½ cup all-purpose flour
½ cup yellow cornmeal
½ teaspoon chili powder
1 cup skim milk
4 eggs, lightly beaten
1 cup (4 ounces) shredded reduced-fat Cheddar cheese
¼ cup nonfat sour cream

Per Serving:
Calories 390
Carbohydrate 57.2g
Protein 23.7g
Fat 8.4g
Fiber 6.0g
Cholesterol 160mg
Sodium 528mg
Calcium 305mg
Exchanges:
3 Grain
2 Vegetable
1½ Medium-Fat Meat

1. Coat a nonstick skillet with cooking spray, and place over medium-high heat until hot. Add green onions, pepper, and garlic; sauté 3 minutes or until tender. Stir in corn and next 5 ingredients; cook until heated. Remove from heat, and keep warm.

2. Combine flour, cornmeal, and chili powder in a medium bowl. Gradually add milk and eggs, stirring with a wire whisk until well blended. Pour mixture evenly into two 9-inch pieplates coated with cooking spray (do not stir). Bake at 475° for 10 minutes or until puffed and browned.

3. Spoon bean mixture evenly into pie shells; sprinkle with cheese. Bake at 475° for 1 minute or until cheese melts. Cut each pie into 6 pieces. Dollop with sour cream. Serve immediately. Yield: 6 servings.

Cajun Beans and Rice Casserole

Time: Prep 28 minutes; Cook 30 minutes

Per Serving:
Calories 266
Carbohydrate 44.2g
Protein 11.0g
Fat 5.4g
Fiber 5.7g
Cholesterol 15mg
Sodium 259mg
Calcium 158mg
Exchanges:
2 Grain
2 Vegetable
1 Lean Meat

1 (16-ounce) can red beans, drained
1 (15-ounce) can no-salt-added pinto beans, drained
1 (14½-ounce) can no-salt-added stewed tomatoes, undrained
Vegetable cooking spray
2 cups chopped onion
½ cup chopped celery
½ cup chopped green pepper
1 teaspoon dried thyme
½ teaspoon dried oregano
½ teaspoon black pepper
¼ teaspoon salt
¼ teaspoon onion powder
⅛ teaspoon ground white pepper
3 cups cooked long-grain rice (cooked without salt or fat)
1 (8-ounce) carton low-fat sour cream
½ cup (2 ounces) shredded reduced-fat Cheddar cheese

1. Mash beans slightly with a fork. Combine beans and tomatoes in a medium saucepan; bring to a boil. Reduce heat; simmer, uncovered, 25 minutes or until most of liquid evaporates.

2. Meanwhile, coat a large nonstick skillet with cooking spray; place over medium-high heat until hot. Add onion, celery, and green pepper; sauté 4 minutes or until tender. Add thyme and next 5 ingredients; cook 5 minutes, stirring often. Stir half of onion mixture into bean mixture.

3. Combine remaining onion mixture, rice, and sour cream. Spoon half of rice mixture into an 11- x 7- x 1½-inch baking dish coated with cooking spray; top with half of bean mixture. Repeat layers with remaining rice and bean mixtures.

4. Cover and bake at 325° for 25 minutes. Uncover and sprinkle with cheese. Bake, uncovered, 5 additional minutes or until cheese melts. Let stand 5 minutes before serving. Yield: 8 servings.

Wild Rice Pilaf

Time: Prep 10 minutes; Cook 30 minutes

1½	cups frozen whole-kernel corn, thawed
2	teaspoons vegetable oil
3	shallots, thinly sliced
	Vegetable cooking spray
1	(6-ounce) package long-grain-and-wild rice mix
½	cup dried apricots, cut into thin strips
2	tablespoons chopped fresh parsley
1	(15-ounce) can no-salt-added garbanzo beans, drained
2	tablespoons balsamic vinegar
2	tablespoons unsweetened orange juice
⅛	teaspoon pepper

Per Serving:
Calories 263
Carbohydrate 52.6g
Protein 9.0g
Fat 2.9g
Fiber 5.5g
Cholesterol 0mg
Sodium 170mg
Calcium 44mg
Exchanges:
2½ Grain
1 Fruit

1. Combine first 3 ingredients in a 2-quart casserole coated with cooking spray, tossing gently. Bake, uncovered, at 375° for 30 to 35 minutes or until vegetables are tender, stirring occasionally.

2. Meanwhile, cook rice according to package directions, omitting fat and half of contents of seasoning packet.

3. Add rice, apricot, parsley, and beans to corn mixture; stir well. Combine vinegar, orange juice, and pepper. Drizzle vinegar mixture over rice mixture; toss gently. Serve immediately. Yield: 6 (1-cup) servings.

I use only half the seasoning packet from the rice mix to reduce the sodium in Wild Rice Pilaf without sacrificing the flavor. It's so flavorful, you won't even miss the salt.

Caramelized Onion Pizza

Time: Prep 15 minutes; Cook 18 minutes

Per Serving:
Calories 271
Carbohydrate 35.1g
Protein 15.7g
Fat 8.5g
Fiber 1.4g
Cholesterol 18mg
Sodium 512mg
Calcium 221mg
Exchanges:
2 Grain
1 Vegetable
1 Medium-Fat Meat

2	tablespoons reduced-calorie margarine
2	cups thinly sliced yellow onion (about 2 medium)
2	tablespoons sugar
1¼	cups lite ricotta cheese
¾	cup (3 ounces) shredded part-skim mozzarella cheese
¼	cup grated Parmesan cheese
2	teaspoons Italian seasoning, divided
⅛	teaspoon pepper
1	(11-ounce) package refrigerated French bread dough
	Vegetable cooking spray
1	large tomato, seeded and thinly sliced
¼	cup chopped fresh parsley

1. Melt margarine in a large skillet over medium-high heat. Add onion and sugar; sauté 5 minutes or until onion is deep golden, stirring often. Set aside.

2. Combine cheeses, 1 teaspoon Italian seasoning, and pepper in a bowl; stir well.

3. Unroll bread dough, and pat into a 13- x 9- x 2-inch baking pan coated with cooking spray. Spread ricotta cheese mixture evenly over dough; top with tomato. Sprinkle with remaining 1 teaspoon Italian seasoning and parsley. Bake, uncovered, at 450° for 13 minutes. Top with onion mixture, and bake 5 additional minutes. Yield: 6 servings.

For pizza in a hurry, split a loaf of French bread in half lengthwise, and lightly toast. For the sauce, combine an 8-ounce can of no-salt-added tomato sauce, 2 teaspoons dried Italian seasoning, and ⅛ teaspoon salt. Pile on your favorite toppings (Canadian bacon, mushrooms, green pepper, onion, fat-free mozzarella cheese, or Parmesan cheese); then bake at 450° for 5 minutes.

Pizza Milanese

Time: Prep 7 minutes; Chill 30 minutes; Cook 15 minutes

1   (9-ounce) package frozen artichoke hearts, thawed and
     coarsely chopped
3   tablespoons commercial fat-free Italian dressing
½   cup lite ricotta cheese
⅓   cup crumbled feta cheese
2   tablespoons nonfat sour cream
⅛   teaspoon hot sauce
2   cloves garlic, minced
1   (16-ounce) Italian bread shell
2   plum tomatoes, thinly sliced
1   yellow tomato, thinly sliced
⅛   teaspoon paprika
¼   teaspoon cracked pepper

Per Serving:
Calories 272
Carbohydrate 41.2g
Protein 13.2g
Fat 6.0g
Fiber 1.8g
Cholesterol 14mg
Sodium 558mg
Calcium 122mg
Exchanges:
2 Grain
1 Vegetable
1 Medium-Fat Meat

1. Combine artichoke and Italian dressing; toss gently. Cover and chill at least 30 minutes; drain.

2. Combine artichoke mixture, ricotta cheese, and next 4 ingredients, stirring well. Spread evenly over bread shell. Arrange tomato slices over artichoke mixture. Sprinkle with paprika and pepper. Bake at 450° for 15 to 18 minutes or until thoroughly heated. Yield: 6 servings.

Spinach Manicotti

Time: Prep 18 minutes; Cook 30 minutes

Per Serving:
Calories 369
Carbohydrate 47.9g
Protein 25.7g
Fat 10.3g
Fiber 6.9g
Cholesterol 23mg
Sodium 705mg
Calcium 396mg
Exchanges:
2 Grain
2 Vegetable
3 Lean Meat

1   (10-ounce) package frozen chopped spinach
8   manicotti shells, uncooked
     Olive oil-flavored vegetable cooking spray
2   teaspoons olive oil
2/3 cup finely chopped onion
2   cloves garlic, minced
1/2 cup freshly grated Parmesan cheese, divided
1/4 teaspoon dried crushed red pepper
1/8 teaspoon ground nutmeg
2   egg whites
1   (15-ounce) carton lite ricotta cheese
2   cups fat-free spaghetti sauce

1. Cook spinach according to package directions, omitting salt. Drain spinach, and press gently between paper towels to remove excess moisture. Set aside.

2. Cook manicotti shells according to package directions, omitting salt and fat; drain well.

3. Meanwhile, coat a medium saucepan with cooking spray; add oil. Place over medium-high heat until hot. Add onion and garlic; sauté 8 minutes. Transfer to a bowl. Add spinach, 1/4 cup Parmesan cheese, and next 4 ingredients; stir well. Stuff mixture evenly into cooked shells.

4. Spread 1/2 cup spaghetti sauce over bottom of a 13- x 9- x 2-inch baking dish. Place filled shells over sauce. Pour remaining spaghetti sauce over shells.

5. Cover; bake at 375° for 30 minutes or until thoroughly heated. Sprinkle with remaining 1/4 cup Parmesan cheese. Yield: 4 servings.

Spicy Chili Mac

Time: Prep 8 minutes; Cook 29 minutes

7	ounces wagon wheel pasta, uncooked
	Vegetable cooking spray
1½	cups finely chopped onion
1⅓	cups finely chopped green pepper
2	cloves garlic, minced
1	tablespoon chili powder
1	teaspoon ground cumin
½	teaspoon garlic powder
½	teaspoon dried crushed red pepper
1	(28-ounce) can crushed tomatoes with puree, undrained
½	pound firm tofu, drained and crumbled
2	(15-ounce) cans kidney beans, drained
¼	cup plus 3 tablespoons (1¾ ounces) shredded reduced-fat Cheddar cheese

Per Serving:
Calories 310
Carbohydrate 50.5g
Protein 18.1g
Fat 5.4g
Fiber 5.7g
Cholesterol 4mg
Sodium 205mg
Calcium 196mg
Exchanges:
2½ Grain
2 Vegetable
1 Lean Meat

1. Cook pasta according to package directions, omitting salt and fat; drain.

2. Meanwhile, coat a Dutch oven with cooking spray; place over medium-high heat until hot. Add onion, green pepper, and garlic; sauté until tender.

3. Add chili powder and next 3 ingredients; sauté 1 minute. Stir in tomatoes and tofu. Bring to a boil; reduce heat, and simmer, uncovered, 15 minutes. Add beans, and cook 10 additional minutes or until thoroughly heated.

4. To serve, place ½ cup pasta in each of seven individual serving bowls, and spoon 1 cup chili over pasta. Top evenly with cheese. Yield: 7 servings.

Spicy Chili Mac

Baked Vegetable Macaroni and Cheese

Time: Prep 19 minutes; Cook 30 minutes

Per Serving:
Calories 230
Carbohydrate 35.4g
Protein 12.8g
Fat 4.2g
Fiber 2.2g
Cholesterol 10mg
Sodium 261mg
Calcium 262mg
Exchanges:
1½ Grain
1 Vegetable
1 Medium-Fat Meat

9   ounces elbow macaroni, uncooked
       Vegetable cooking spray
1   teaspoon vegetable oil
¾   cup chopped onion
2   cloves garlic, minced
2   cups small broccoli flowerets
1   cup seeded, coarsely chopped tomato
¼   cup chopped fresh basil
¼   cup chopped fresh parsley
⅓   cup all-purpose flour
½   teaspoon salt
⅛   teaspoon pepper
2½   cups skim milk
½   cup (2 ounces) shredded reduced-fat Cheddar cheese
½   cup (2 ounces) shredded reduced-fat Swiss cheese

1. Cook macaroni according to package directions, omitting salt and fat; drain and set aside.

2. Meanwhile, coat a large nonstick skillet with cooking spray; add oil, and place over medium-high heat until hot. Add onion and garlic; sauté 3 minutes. Add broccoli; sauté 1 minute or until vegetables are crisp-tender. Stir in tomato, basil, and parsley; set aside.

3. Combine flour, salt, and pepper in a medium saucepan. Gradually add milk, stirring until smooth. Cook over medium heat, stirring constantly, until mixture is thickened and bubbly.

4. Add cheeses to milk mixture, stirring until smooth. Stir in macaroni and vegetable mixture. Spoon into a 2-quart baking dish coated with cooking spray. Bake at 350° for 30 minutes. Yield: 8 servings.

Southwestern Pasta Toss

Time: Prep 5 minutes; Cook 12 minutes

4	ounces rotini (corkscrew pasta), uncooked
1¾	cups no-salt-added chunky salsa
	Vegetable cooking spray
1	teaspoon olive oil
½	teaspoon ground cumin
1	clove garlic, minced
1	cup frozen whole-kernel corn, thawed
1	(15-ounce) can black beans, drained
¼	cup chopped fresh cilantro
2	tablespoons grated Parmesan cheese
1	tablespoon lime juice

Per Serving:
Calories 300
Carbohydrate 56.1g
Protein 13.1g
Fat 3.7g
Fiber 5.4g
Cholesterol 2mg
Sodium 221mg
Calcium 136mg
Exchanges:
3 Grain
1 Vegetable
1 Lean Meat

1. Cook pasta according to package directions, omitting salt and fat; drain. Place pasta in a serving bowl. Add salsa, and toss gently.

2. Coat a medium nonstick skillet with cooking spray; add oil. Place over medium heat until hot. Add cumin and garlic; sauté 30 seconds. Stir in corn and beans. Cook, stirring constantly, until thoroughly heated. Add corn mixture, cilantro, cheese, and lime juice to pasta mixture; toss mixture gently. Serve immediately. Yield: 4 (1¼-cup) servings.

To create a more pronounced flavor, I stir dried spices like cumin in a hot skillet to toast them (with or without oil) for a few minutes.

Garden Orecchiette

Time: Prep 15 minutes; Cook 12 minutes

Per Serving:
Calories 241
Carbohydrate 40.6g
Protein 11.2g
Fat 3.9g
Fiber 3.8g
Cholesterol 11mg
Sodium 350mg
Calcium 143mg
Exchanges:
2 Grain
2 Vegetable
1 Medium-Fat Meat

10	ounces fresh asparagus
12	ounces orecchiette pasta, uncooked
1	(14½-ounce) can vegetable broth
1½	cups julienne-sliced sweet yellow pepper
1	cup diagonally sliced carrot
2	cups Sugar Snap peas, trimmed
1	cup frozen English peas
¼	cup chopped fresh chives
2	tablespoons chopped fresh basil
1	tablespoon chopped fresh thyme
⅛	teaspoon salt
¾	cup grated Romano cheese
	Freshly ground pepper (optional)

1. Snap off tough ends of asparagus. Remove scales from stalks with a knife or vegetable peeler, if desired. Cut asparagus into 1-inch pieces, and set aside.

2. Cook pasta according to package directions, omitting salt and fat; drain well.

3. Meanwhile, bring vegetable broth to a boil in a large saucepan. Add asparagus, yellow pepper, and carrot. Reduce heat; simmer, uncovered, 4 minutes. Add peas, and cook 3 additional minutes or until vegetables are crisp-tender. Add chives and next 3 ingredients.

4. Place pasta in a serving bowl. Add vegetable mixture; toss well. Add ½ cup cheese; toss well. Sprinkle with remaining ¼ cup cheese. Sprinkle with ground pepper, if desired. Yield: 8 (¾-cup) servings.

Note: Orecchiette is a small bowl-shaped pasta. You can substitute the same weight of a different shape of pasta, if desired.

Fresh Pepper Pasta

Time: Prep 7 minutes; Cook 33 minutes

4	medium-size sweet red peppers (about 1½ pounds), seeded and chopped
2	tablespoons dry white wine
¾	cup drained canned navy beans
½	cup thinly sliced green onions
¼	cup plus 2 tablespoons chopped fresh basil
1	tablespoon minced fresh oregano
1	tablespoon chopped ripe olives
6	ounces rotini (corkscrew pasta), uncooked
¼	cup plus 2 tablespoons (1½ ounces) grated Asiago or Parmesan cheese
1	tablespoon pine nuts, toasted
	Fresh basil sprigs (optional)

Per Serving:
Calories 284
Carbohydrate 47.3g
Protein 12.8g
Fat 5.7g
Fiber 3.7g
Cholesterol 5mg
Sodium 294mg
Calcium 201mg
Exchanges:
2½ Grain
1 Vegetable
1 Medium-Fat Meat

1. Combine red pepper and wine in a saucepan; bring to a boil. Cover, reduce heat, and simmer 3 minutes.

2. Stir in beans and next 4 ingredients; bring to a boil. Cover, reduce heat, and simmer 10 minutes. Uncover and simmer 20 minutes, stirring occasionally.

3. Meanwhile, cook pasta according to package directions, omitting salt and fat. Drain well.

4. Place pasta on individual serving plates. Top with pepper mixture, cheese, and pine nuts. Garnish with basil sprigs, if desired. Yield: 4 (1½-cup) servings.

Fresh Pepper Pasta

Cheese-Stuffed Potatoes

Cheese-Stuffed Potatoes

Time: Prep 12 minutes; Cook 1 hour and 15 minutes

Per Serving:
Calories 280
Carbohydrate 48.7g
Protein 12.7g
Fat 3.3g
Fiber 3.3g
Cholesterol 11mg
Sodium 272mg
Calcium 168mg
Exchanges:
3 Grain
½ Lean Meat

6 small baking potatoes (about 1¼ pounds)
¾ cup plus 2 tablespoons shredded reduced-fat sharp
    Cheddar cheese
1½ cups nonfat sour cream
⅓ cup finely chopped green onions
¼ teaspoon salt
    Paprika

1. Bake potatoes at 400° for 1 hour or until done; let cool slightly. Cut a ¼-inch-thick slice from the top of each baked potato; carefully scoop pulp into a bowl, leaving shells intact. Add cheese and sour cream to pulp, and mash; stir in green onions and salt.

2. Stuff shells with potato mixture; sprinkle with paprika. Place on a baking sheet, and bake at 450° for 15 minutes or until thoroughly heated. Yield: 6 servings.

Microwave directions: Pierce potatoes with a fork, and arrange in a circle on paper towels in microwave oven. Microwave at HIGH 16 minutes or until done, turning and rearranging potatoes halfway through cooking time. Let stand 5 minutes. Stuff potatoes as directed above; microwave at HIGH 5 minutes or until thoroughly heated.

Meats, Poultry & Seafood

Steak Diane (page 141), Scalloped Potatoes (page 199)

Grilled Spicy Flank Steak

Time: Prep 15 minutes; Cook 12 minutes

Per Serving:
Calories 416
Carbohydrate 42.5g
Protein 28.1g
Fat 13.7g
Fiber 2.2g
Cholesterol 60mg
Sodium 518mg
Calcium 30mg
Exchanges:
3 Grain
3 Lean Meat

¼ cup hoisin sauce
1 tablespoon molasses
1 teaspoon Chinese chili puree with garlic
½ teaspoon salt-free lemon-pepper seasoning
1 (1½-pound) lean flank steak
Vegetable cooking spray
6 cups cooked capellini (cooked without salt or fat)
½ cup sliced green onions
2 tablespoons low-sodium soy sauce

1. Combine first 4 ingredients; set aside.

2. Trim fat from steak. Coat grill rack with cooking spray; place on grill over medium-hot coals (350° to 400°). Place steak on rack; grill, covered, 6 to 7 minutes on each side or to desired degree of doneness, basting often during the last 5 minutes with hoisin sauce mixture. Let steak stand 5 minutes. Cut diagonally across grain into thin slices.

3. Combine pasta, onions, and soy sauce; toss gently. Place mixture on a serving platter. Top with steak slices. Yield: 6 servings.

Hoisin sauce is a thick, sweet, spicy sauce that's available in most grocery stores. However, you can use equal parts of brown sugar and reduced-sodium soy sauce, along with a dash of garlic powder, as a simple substitute.

Beef and Vegetable Kabobs

Time: Prep 10 minutes; Marinate 8 hours; Cook 12 minutes

1	pound lean boneless beef sirloin steak
¼	cup dry red wine
¼	cup reduced-calorie maple syrup
2	tablespoons red wine vinegar
1½	teaspoons olive oil
1	teaspoon minced garlic
1	teaspoon curry powder
½	teaspoon pepper
4	small onions, quartered
2	small sweet red peppers, seeded and cut into 1-inch pieces
2	medium zucchini, each cut into 4 (1-inch) pieces
2	medium-size yellow squash, each cut into 4 (1-inch) pieces
8	medium-size fresh mushrooms
	Vegetable cooking spray

Per Serving:
Calories 290
Carbohydrate 21.3g
Protein 31.1g
Fat 9.8g
Fiber 3.9g
Cholesterol 80mg
Sodium 80mg
Calcium 79mg
Exchanges:
3 Lean Meat
4 Vegetable

1. Trim fat from steak; cut steak into 1-inch pieces. Place steak in a heavy-duty, zip-top plastic bag. Combine wine and next 6 ingredients in a small bowl, stirring well. Pour over steak. Seal bag, and shake until steak is well coated. Marinate in refrigerator at least 8 hours, turning bag occasionally.

2. Remove steak from marinade, reserving marinade. Place marinade in a small saucepan; bring to a boil. Reduce heat, and simmer 2 minutes.

3. Thread steak, onion, and next 4 ingredients alternately onto eight 10-inch skewers. Coat grill rack with cooking spray; place on grill over medium-hot coals (350° to 400°). Place kabobs on rack, and grill, covered, 12 to 14 minutes or to desired degree of doneness, turning and basting often with marinade. Yield: 4 servings.

Jerk Meat Loaf

Time: Prep 6 minutes; Cook 1 hour

1	pound ground round
1	cup soft whole wheat breadcrumbs
½	cup finely chopped green onions
¼	cup fat-free egg substitute
¼	cup skim milk
¼	cup reduced-calorie ketchup
2	tablespoons white vinegar
1	teaspoon dried thyme
½	teaspoon salt
½	teaspoon ground allspice
½	teaspoon coarsely ground pepper
⅛	teaspoon ground nutmeg
⅛	teaspoon ground cinnamon
2	jalapeño peppers, seeded and finely chopped
	Vegetable cooking spray

1. Combine all ingredients except cooking spray in a medium bowl. Shape mixture into an 8- x 4-inch loaf; place on a rack in a roasting pan coated with cooking spray. Bake, uncovered, at 350° for 1 hour. Yield: 6 servings.

"Jerk" is a term for a style of barbecue that includes a mixture of herbs, spices, and the hottest peppers available. For the most flavor, use freshly ground spices. (You can grind whole allspice and nutmeg in a coffee grinder.) For an even more authentic fiery flavor, I substitute Scotch bonnet or habanero chile peppers for the jalapeño peppers.

Steak Diane

Time: Prep 6 minutes; Cook 12 minutes

½ teaspoon coarsely ground pepper
6 (4-ounce) beef tenderloin steaks (1 inch thick)
1 teaspoon margarine
Butter-flavored vegetable cooking spray
1 tablespoon all-purpose flour
¼ cup water
¼ cup dry red wine
2 tablespoons lemon juice
1 tablespoon Worcestershire sauce
2 teaspoons Dijon mustard
1½ teaspoons browning-and-seasoning sauce (such as Kitchen Bouquet)

Per Serving:
Calories 185
Carbohydrate 2.2g
Protein 23.8g
Fat 8.3g
Fiber 0.1g
Cholesterol 70mg
Sodium 144mg
Calcium 12mg
Exchanges:
3 Lean Meat

1. Sprinkle pepper over steaks. Melt margarine in a large nonstick skillet coated with cooking spray over medium-high heat. Add steaks, and cook 5 minutes on each side or to desired degree of doneness. Place steaks on a platter; set aside, and keep warm.

2. Place flour in a small bowl. Gradually add water, stirring until well blended. Add flour mixture, wine, and remaining 4 ingredients to skillet; bring to boil, and cook, stirring constantly, 2 minutes or until reduced to 6 tablespoons. Spoon over steaks. Yield: 6 servings.

Individual Beef Wellingtons

Time: Prep 18 minutes; Cook 15 minutes

Per Serving:
Calories 306
Carbohydrate 22.4g
Protein 27.2g
Fat 11.2g
Fiber 0.7g
Cholesterol 70mg
Sodium 388mg
Calcium 17mg
Exchanges:
1 Grain
1 Vegetable
3½ Lean Meat

Olive oil-flavored vegetable cooking spray
2 cups sliced fresh mushrooms, minced
1 teaspoon minced green onions
¼ teaspoon salt
4 (4-ounce) beef tenderloin steaks
1 teaspoon coarsely ground pepper
8 sheets frozen phyllo pastry, thawed

1. Coat a nonstick skillet with cooking spray, and place over medium-high heat until hot. Add mushrooms, green onions, and salt; sauté 8 minutes. Remove from skillet, and set aside.

2. Sprinkle both sides of each steak with pepper. Coat skillet with cooking spray; place over high heat until hot. Add steaks; cook 1½ minutes on each side or until lightly browned. Remove from skillet; drain on paper towels.

3. Place 1 sheet of phyllo on a damp towel (keeping remaining phyllo covered). Lightly coat phyllo with cooking spray. Top with another sheet of phyllo, and coat with cooking spray; fold in half crosswise, bringing short ends together. Place 1 steak 3 inches from 1 end of phyllo. Spoon one-fourth of mushroom mixture over steak. Fold short end of phyllo over mushroom mixture; fold lengthwise edges of phyllo over steak, and roll up, jellyroll fashion. Repeat procedure with remaining phyllo, mushroom mixture, and steaks.

4. Lightly coat packets with cooking spray; place, seam sides down, on a baking sheet coated with cooking spray. Bake at 425° for 15 minutes or until golden. Serve immediately. Yield: 4 servings.

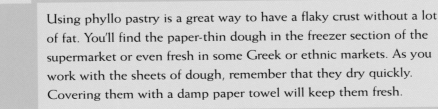

Using phyllo pastry is a great way to have a flaky crust without a lot of fat. You'll find the paper-thin dough in the freezer section of the supermarket or even fresh in some Greek or ethnic markets. As you work with the sheets of dough, remember that they dry quickly. Covering them with a damp paper towel will keep them fresh.

Veal Ragoût

Time: Prep 10 minutes; Cook 1 hour and 19 minutes

2½   pounds lean boneless veal sirloin tip roast
1½   teaspoons paprika
½   teaspoon freshly ground pepper
     Vegetable cooking spray
1   tablespoon olive oil, divided
2½   cups sliced leeks (about 3 large leeks)
3   cloves garlic, minced
⅓   cup all-purpose flour
1½   cups dry vermouth
2   (14¼-ounce) cans no-salt-added chicken
     broth
2   teaspoons dried thyme
2   bay leaves
1   pound carrots, scraped and cut into 2-inch-long strips
½   teaspoon salt
8   cups cooked fettuccine (cooked without salt or fat)
2   tablespoons chopped fresh thyme

Veal Ragoût

1. Trim fat from veal; cut veal into 1-inch cubes. Sprinkle paprika and pepper over veal. Coat an ovenproof Dutch oven with cooking spray; add 1 teaspoon oil. Place over medium-high heat until hot. Add half of veal; cook until browned on all sides, stirring often. Transfer to a bowl; set aside. Repeat with 1 teaspoon oil and remaining veal. Wipe drippings from Dutch oven with a paper towel.

2. Add remaining 1 teaspoon oil to Dutch oven, and place over medium-high heat until hot. Add leeks and garlic; sauté 3 to 4 minutes. Return veal to Dutch oven; sprinkle with flour. Cook, stirring constantly, 1 minute. Stir in vermouth and next 3 ingredients. Bring to a boil; cover and bake at 350° for 30 minutes.

3. Add carrot and salt to veal mixture. Bake, uncovered, 35 to 45 minutes or until veal and carrot are tender. Remove and discard bay leaves. Serve over pasta; sprinkle with chopped thyme. Yield: 8 (1½-cup) servings.

Per Serving:
Calories 439
Carbohydrate 54.3g
Protein 36.1g
Fat 7.2g
Fiber 4.0g
Cholesterol 120mg
Sodium 325mg
Calcium 92mg
Exchanges:
3 Grain
2 Vegetable
3 Lean Meat

Veal with Sour Cream Sauce

Time: Prep 8 minutes; Cook 17 minutes

Per Serving:
Calories 163
Carbohydrate 3.9g
Protein 25.8g
Fat 4.0g
Fiber 0.2g
Cholesterol 88mg
Sodium 235mg
Calcium 13mg
Exchanges:
3 Lean Meat

1	pound lean ground veal
¼	teaspoon salt
¼	teaspoon pepper
	Vegetable cooking spray
¼	cup chopped shallots
⅔	cup canned low-sodium chicken broth, undiluted
2	tablespoons sherry
½	teaspoon paprika
¼	teaspoon freshly ground pepper
¼	cup plus 2 tablespoons nonfat sour cream
1½	tablespoons chopped fresh parsley

1. Combine first 3 ingredients in a small bowl, stirring well. Shape into 4 (½-inch-thick) patties.

2. Coat a large nonstick skillet with cooking spray, and place over medium-high heat until hot. Add veal patties; cook 2 to 3 minutes on each side or until browned. Remove patties from skillet, and keep warm. Add shallots to skillet; sauté 1 minute. Add chicken broth and next 3 ingredients; cook 2 minutes, stirring occasionally. Return veal patties to skillet; cook, covered, over low heat 10 minutes or until veal is no longer pink. Transfer veal to a serving platter, and keep warm.

3. Pour broth mixture in skillet through a wire-mesh strainer into a small bowl, reserving ¼ cup. Discard remaining broth mixture and solids. Add sour cream to reserved broth mixture; stir to blend. Spoon over patties, and sprinkle with parsley. Yield: 4 servings.

Lamb Chops with Cherry Sauce

Time: Prep 10 minutes; Cook 22 minutes

4	(5-ounce) lean lamb loin chops (1 inch thick)
½	teaspoon cracked pepper
	Olive oil-flavored vegetable cooking spray
1	cup coarsely chopped onion
½	cup chopped celery
1	clove garlic, minced
1	cup dry red wine
1	cup canned no-salt-added beef broth, undiluted
2	tablespoons red currant jelly
1	teaspoon dried thyme
½	teaspoon pepper
¼	teaspoon salt
⅛	teaspoon ground cinnamon
1	tablespoon cornstarch
1	tablespoon water
2	cups frozen pitted sweet cherries, halved

Per Serving:
Calories 304
Carbohydrate 21.5g
Protein 30.8g
Fat 10.1g
Fiber 1.4g
Cholesterol 93mg
Sodium 256mg
Calcium 59mg
Exchanges:
1 Fruit
1 Vegetable
4 Lean Meat

1. Trim fat from chops; sprinkle with cracked pepper. Coat a large nonstick skillet with cooking spray; place over medium heat until hot. Add chops; cover and cook 4 minutes on each side or until browned. Uncover; cook 5 minutes on each side or to desired degree of doneness. Remove chops from skillet; keep warm. Wipe drippings from skillet with a paper towel.

2. Coat skillet with cooking spray; place over medium-high heat until hot. Add onion, celery, and garlic; sauté until crisp-tender. Add wine and broth; bring to a boil. Cook 5 minutes or until reduced by half. Pour through a wire-mesh strainer into a bowl; discard vegetables remaining in strainer.

Lamb Chops with Cherry Sauce

3. Return wine mixture to skillet; add jelly and next 4 ingredients. Cook over low heat until jelly melts, stirring often. Combine cornstarch and water in a bowl; add to wine mixture. Cook over medium heat, stirring constantly, until thickened and bubbly. Add chops and cherries; cook until thoroughly heated. Yield: 4 servings.

Red Currant-Glazed Pork Chops

Time: Prep 5 minutes; Cook 16 minutes

Per Serving:
Calories 234
Carbohydrate 13.7g
Protein 25.1g
Fat 8.3g
Fiber 0.2g
Cholesterol 71mg
Sodium 375mg
Calcium 12mg
Exchanges:
1 Fruit
3 Lean Meat

4 (4-ounce) lean boneless center-cut loin pork chops (about ½ inch thick)
¾ teaspoon rubbed sage
½ teaspoon salt
¼ teaspoon pepper
   Vegetable cooking spray
¼ cup red currant jelly
2 tablespoons balsamic vinegar

1. Trim fat from chops. Sprinkle sage, salt, and pepper over both sides of chops.

2. Coat a medium nonstick skillet with cooking spray; place over medium heat until hot. Add chops, and cook 7 minutes on each side or until done. Remove from skillet; place on a serving platter, and keep warm.

3. Add jelly and vinegar to skillet; cook 2 minutes or until thickened and bubbly, stirring constantly. Spoon over chops. Yield: 4 servings.

Peppercorn-Crusted Pork Loin Roast

Time: Prep 8 minutes; Cook 2 hours; Stand 10 minutes

Per Serving:
Calories 241
Carbohydrate 10.0g
Protein 26.7g
Fat 10.1g
Fiber 0.8g
Cholesterol 70mg
Sodium 478mg
Calcium 80mg
Exchanges:
½ Grain
3½ Lean Meat

1 (2½-pound) lean boneless pork loin roast
3 tablespoons Dijon mustard
1 tablespoon nonfat buttermilk
2 cups soft whole wheat breadcrumbs
2 tablespoons cracked pepper
2 teaspoons whole assorted peppercorns, crushed
2 teaspoons chopped fresh thyme
¼ teaspoon salt
   Vegetable cooking spray
   Creamy Peppercorn Sauce
   Fresh thyme sprigs (optional)

1. Trim fat from roast. Combine mustard and buttermilk; spread over roast.

2. Combine bread-crumbs and next 4 ingredients; press evenly onto roast. Place roast on a rack in a roasting pan coated with cooking spray. Insert a meat thermometer into thickest part of roast, if desired. Bake at 325° for 2 hours or until meat thermometer registers 160°. Let stand 10 minutes before slicing. Serve with Creamy Peppercorn Sauce. Garnish with thyme sprigs, if desired. Yield: 10 servings.

Peppercorn-Crusted Pork Loin Roast

Creamy Peppercorn Sauce

- ¾ cup nonfat buttermilk
- ⅓ cup nonfat sour cream
- 3 tablespoons grated Parmesan cheese
- 3 tablespoons reduced-fat mayonnaise
- 1½ tablespoons lemon juice
- 1½ teaspoons whole assorted peppercorns, crushed
- ¼ teaspoon salt

1. Combine all ingredients in a small bowl, stirring well. Yield: 1¼ cups plus 1 tablespoon.

A **meat thermometer** is the most accurate guide for checking the doneness of a roast. Insert the thermometer into the surface of the meat at a slight angle; the tip of the thermometer should be in the thickest portion of the meat but should not rest in fat or against a bone. **Instant-read thermometers** can also be used by sticking the thermometer into the cooked meat. Instant-read thermometers should be used only for a quick read and should not be kept in the meat during baking.

Chicken Fried Rice

Time: Prep 5 minutes; Cook 12 minutes

Per Serving:
Calories 270
Carbohydrate 26.8g
Protein 24.6g
Fat 6.2g
Fiber 0.8g
Cholesterol 108mg
Sodium 376mg
Calcium 34mg
Exchanges:
1½ Grain
3 Lean Meat

1 egg, lightly beaten
⅓ cup canned no-salt-added chicken broth, undiluted
2 tablespoons reduced-sodium soy sauce
½ teaspoon pepper
Vegetable cooking spray
2 teaspoons peanut oil
½ cup finely chopped fresh mushrooms
¼ cup thinly sliced green onions
2 cups hot cooked long-grain rice (cooked without salt or fat)
2 cups chopped cooked chicken breast (skinned before cooking and cooked without salt)

1. Combine first 4 ingredients; stir well. Set aside.

2. Coat a wok or nonstick skillet with cooking spray; add oil. Heat at medium-high (375°) until hot. Add mushrooms and onions; stir-fry 3 minutes. Stir in rice and chicken. Cook, stirring constantly, 6 to 8 minutes or until thoroughly heated. Drizzle egg mixture over rice and chicken mixture, stirring constantly, until egg is soft-cooked. Serve warm. Yield: 4 servings.

Chicken and Vegetable Lo Mein

Time: Prep 10 minutes; Cook 12 minutes

6	ounces vermicelli, uncooked
2	(4-ounce) skinned, boned chicken breast halves, cut into thin strips
½	teaspoon dried crushed red pepper
2	cloves garlic, minced
	Vegetable cooking spray
2	teaspoons dark sesame oil, divided
3	cups sliced bok choy
¾	cup canned low-sodium chicken broth, undiluted
2	tablespoons low-sodium soy sauce
1	tablespoon oyster sauce
½	cup coarsely shredded carrot
⅓	cup diagonally sliced green onions
2	teaspoons sesame seeds, toasted

Per Serving:
Calories 282
Carbohydrate 36.7g
Protein 20.8g
Fat 5.2g
Fiber 2.3g
Cholesterol 33mg
Sodium 439mg
Calcium 84mg
Exchanges:
2 Grain
1 Vegetable
2 Lean Meat

1. Cook pasta according to package directions, omitting salt and fat; drain and set aside.

2. Meanwhile, combine chicken, red pepper, and garlic, tossing well. Coat a wok or large nonstick skillet with cooking spray; drizzle 1 teaspoon oil around top of wok, coating sides. Heat at medium-high (375°) until hot. Add chicken mixture; stir-fry 2 minutes. Add bok choy; stir-fry 2 minutes. Add broth, soy sauce, and oyster sauce; stir-fry 1 minute. Add carrot and green onions; stir-fry 1 minute.

3. Add cooked pasta and remaining 1 teaspoon oil to wok; toss gently until thoroughly heated. Sprinkle with sesame seeds. Serve immediately. Yield: 4 (1¼-cup) servings.

> Bok choy is a Chinese vegetable with white stalks and dark green leaves. I've found that you can store it in an airtight container in the refrigerator for about four days.

Moroccan Chicken and Orzo

Moroccan Chicken and Orzo

Time: Prep 11 minutes; Cook 16 minutes

Per Serving:
Calories 327
Carbohydrate 43.4g
Protein 27.8g
Fat 4.3g
Fiber 2.4g
Cholesterol 53mg
Sodium 199mg
Calcium 39mg
Exchanges:
2 Grain
3 Lean Meat

1 cup orzo, uncooked
1 teaspoon paprika
½ teaspoon ground cumin
¼ teaspoon salt
¼ teaspoon saffron threads or ⅛ teaspoon ground turmeric
⅛ teaspoon ground cinnamon
1 clove garlic, minced
4 (4-ounce) skinned, boned chicken breast halves, cut into
  1-inch pieces
Vegetable cooking spray
2 teaspoons vegetable oil
1¼ cups chopped onion
1 cup canned low-sodium chicken broth
¼ cup golden raisins
¼ cup chopped fresh cilantro
Fresh cilantro leaves (optional)

1. Cook orzo according to package directions, omitting salt and fat; drain.

2. Meanwhile, combine paprika and next 5 ingredients in a medium bowl. Add chicken, tossing to coat.

3. Coat a nonstick skillet with cooking spray; add oil. Place over medium-high heat until hot. Add onion; sauté 4 minutes. Add chicken mixture, and cook 6 minutes or until chicken is browned, stirring often. Add broth and raisins; reduce heat to medium, and cook 5 minutes.

4. Add orzo to skillet, stirring until heated. Spoon into individual serving bowls. Sprinkle with chopped cilantro. Garnish with cilantro leaves, if desired. Yield: 5 (1-cup) servings.

Poached Ginger Chicken

Time: Prep 10 minutes; Cook 20 minutes; Chill 1 hour

4   (4-ounce) skinned, boned chicken breast halves
2   cups water
    Vegetable cooking spray
1   teaspoon peanut oil
¾   cup chopped green onions
¼   cup peeled, grated gingerroot
2   tablespoons dark brown sugar
2   tablespoons dry sherry
2   tablespoons low-sodium soy sauce
    Boston lettuce leaves (optional)
    Green onions (optional)

Per Serving:
Calories 187
Carbohydrate 7.8g
Protein 26.9g
Fat 4.4g
Fiber 0.4g
Cholesterol 72mg
Sodium 264mg
Calcium 29mg
Exchanges:
1 Vegetable
3 Lean Meat

1. Combine chicken and water in a large saucepan. Bring to a boil; cover, reduce heat, and simmer 20 minutes or until chicken is done. Remove chicken from broth; discard broth. Cut chicken into thin slices; place slices in a shallow baking dish.

2. Coat a small nonstick skillet with cooking spray; add oil. Place over medium-high heat until hot. Add chopped green onions and gingerroot; sauté 30 seconds. Remove from heat, and spoon over chicken.

3. Add sugar, sherry, and soy sauce to skillet; bring to a boil. Boil 1 minute. Pour over chicken. Cover and chill thoroughly. If desired, spoon chicken mixture onto individual lettuce-lined plates, and garnish with green onions. Yield: 4 servings.

Parmesan Chicken with Tomato Cream Sauce

Time: Prep 15 minutes; Cook 30 minutes

Per Serving:
Calories 387
Carbohydrate 45.8g
Protein 37.0g
Fat 5.3g
Fiber 1.4g
Cholesterol 71mg
Sodium 446mg
Calcium 218mg
Exchanges:
2 Grain
2 Vegetable
3 Lean Meat

¼	cup 1% low-fat milk
1	tablespoon Dijon mustard
½	cup fine, dry breadcrumbs
2	tablespoons grated Parmesan cheese
½	teaspoon dried Italian seasoning
⅛	teaspoon garlic powder
⅛	teaspoon pepper
6	(4-ounce) skinned, boned chicken breast halves
	Vegetable cooking spray
8	ounces linguine, uncooked
	Tomato Cream Sauce
	Fresh basil sprigs (optional)

1. Combine milk and mustard, stirring with a wire whisk. Combine breadcrumbs and next 4 ingredients in a bowl. Dip chicken in milk mixture; dredge in breadcrumb mixture. Place chicken on a baking sheet coated with cooking spray. Bake at 375° for 30 minutes or until golden.

2. Cook pasta according to package directions, omitting salt and fat; drain. Place 1 cup linguine on each serving plate; top with chicken and Tomato Cream Sauce. Garnish with basil sprigs, if desired. Yield: 6 servings.

Tomato Cream Sauce

1	teaspoon olive oil
3	cloves garlic, minced
2	(14½-ounce) cans no-salt-added whole tomatoes, undrained and crushed
1	tablespoon chopped fresh basil
1	tablespoon chopped fresh oregano
2	teaspoons chopped fresh parsley
¼	teaspoon sugar
¼	teaspoon salt
1	cup 1% low-fat milk
1	tablespoon all-purpose flour
2	tablespoons grated Parmesan cheese

1. Heat oil in a medium saucepan over medium-high heat until hot. Add garlic; sauté until tender. Add tomato and next 5 ingredients; bring mixture to a boil. Reduce heat, and simmer, uncovered, 20 minutes, stirring occasionally.

2. Combine milk and flour in a small bowl, stirring well with a wire whisk. Gradually add milk mixture to tomato mixture, stirring constantly. Cook, stirring constantly, 5 minutes or until slightly thickened. Stir in cheese. Yield: 4 cups.

Parmesan Chicken with Tomato Cream Sauce

Garlic-Ginger Chicken

Time: Prep 5 minutes; Cook 45 minutes

1	teaspoon peeled, grated gingerroot
2	teaspoons rice wine vinegar
2	teaspoons ketchup
1	teaspoon water
¼	teaspoon salt
¼	teaspoon ground cinnamon
¼	teaspoon ground cardamom
¼	teaspoon ground red pepper
4	cloves garlic, minced
4	(6-ounce) skinned chicken breast halves
	Vegetable cooking spray

Per Serving:
Calories 152
Carbohydrate 2.2g
Protein 26.7g
Fat 3.2g
Fiber 0.2g
Cholesterol 72mg
Sodium 240mg
Calcium 22mg
Exchanges:
3 Lean Meat

1. Combine first 9 ingredients in a small bowl, stirring well.

2. Place chicken, skinned side up, on a rack in a roasting pan coated with cooking spray. Brush ketchup mixture over chicken. Bake at 375° for 45 minutes or until chicken is done, turning and basting chicken occasionally with ketchup mixture. Yield: 4 servings.

Chicken Breasts with Marmalade

Chicken Breasts with Marmalade

Time: Prep 9 minutes; Cook 25 minutes

Per Serving:
Calories 258
Carbohydrate 25.6g
Protein 30.7g
Fat 3.0g
Fiber 1.5g
Cholesterol 66mg
Sodium 481mg
Calcium 21mg
Exchanges:
1 Grain
1 Vegetable
3 Lean Meat

Vegetable cooking spray
1 teaspoon margarine
½ cup finely chopped onion
4 large fresh crimini mushrooms, sliced
⅛ teaspoon salt
⅛ teaspoon pepper
4 (6-ounce) skinned chicken breast halves
¼ cup water
¼ cup low-sodium teriyaki sauce
2 tablespoons low-sugar orange marmalade
2 cups cooked couscous (cooked without salt or fat)
Orange slices (optional)
Flat-leaf parsley sprigs (optional)

1. Coat a large nonstick skillet with cooking spray; add margarine. Place over medium-high heat until margarine melts. Add onion and mushrooms; sauté until tender. Transfer to a small bowl. Stir in salt and pepper; set aside.

2. Coat skillet with cooking spray; place over medium-high heat until hot. Add chicken, and cook 2 minutes on each side or until browned. Combine water, teriyaki sauce, and marmalade; pour over chicken. Bring to a boil; cover, reduce heat, and simmer 20 minutes or until chicken is done, turning occasionally. Add mushroom mixture; bring to a boil. Reduce heat; simmer, uncovered, 3 minutes.

3. To serve, place ½ cup couscous on each individual serving plate. Top with chicken breasts. Spoon mushroom mixture over chicken. If desired, garnish with orange slices and parsley sprigs. Yield: 4 servings.

Lemon Chicken and Potatoes

Time: Prep 5 minutes; Cook 1 hour

	Vegetable cooking spray
3	large baking potatoes, peeled and cut crosswise into ½-inch-thick slices
1	cup canned no-salt-added chicken broth
½	cup dry white wine
¼	cup fresh lemon juice
8	cloves garlic, minced
6	(6-ounce) skinned chicken breast halves
1	tablespoon olive oil
½	teaspoon salt
½	teaspoon freshly ground pepper
12	thin slices lemon

Per Serving:
Calories 297
Carbohydrate 34.3g
Protein 30.2g
Fat 4.0g
Fiber 2.9g
Cholesterol 66mg
Sodium 283mg
Calcium 36mg
Exchanges:
2 Grain
3 Lean Meat

1. Coat a 13- x 9- x 2-inch pan with cooking spray. Arrange potato in pan. Combine broth and next 3 ingredients; pour half of broth mixture over potato. Bake, uncovered, at 375° for 15 minutes.

2. Add chicken to pan, and pour remaining broth mixture over chicken and potato. Brush chicken with oil. Sprinkle with salt and pepper. Top each chicken breast with 2 lemon slices. Bake, uncovered, 45 additional minutes or until chicken is done and potato is tender, basting often with pan juices. Yield: 6 servings.

Crispy Drumsticks

Time: Prep 8 minutes; Cook 40 minutes

Per Serving:
Calories 198
Carbohydrate 5.3g
Protein 28.8g
Fat 5.9g
Fiber 0.3g
Cholesterol 89mg
Sodium 164mg
Calcium 26mg
Exchanges:
½ Grain
3 Lean Meat

¼   cup fine, dry breadcrumbs
⅛   teaspoon garlic powder
⅛   teaspoon onion powder
⅛   teaspoon dried whole marjoram
⅛   teaspoon dried whole thyme
1   egg white, lightly beaten
1   tablespoon skim milk
8   chicken drumsticks, skinned (about 1½ pounds)
    Vegetable cooking spray

1. Combine first 5 ingredients in a shallow dish; stir well. Combine egg white and milk in a small bowl. Dip each drumstick in milk mixture; dredge in breadcrumb mixture.

2. Place drumsticks in a 13- x 9- x 2-inch baking dish coated with cooking spray. Bake, uncovered, at 350° for 40 to 45 minutes or until done. Yield: 4 servings.

Turkey Enchiladas

Time: Prep 14 minutes; Cook 25 minutes

Per Serving:
Calories 349
Carbohydrate 39.7g
Protein 34.2g
Fat 6.0g
Fiber 5.1g
Cholesterol 63mg
Sodium 703mg
Calcium 474mg
Exchanges:
1½ Grain
3 Vegetable
3 Lean Meat

1   pound freshly ground raw turkey breast
2   cups no-salt-added salsa, divided
1   (10-ounce) package frozen chopped spinach, thawed and
     drained
1   (8-ounce) package nonfat cream cheese, cubed
12 (6-inch) corn tortillas
    Vegetable cooking spray
1   (14½-ounce) can no-salt-added whole tomatoes,
     undrained and chopped
1   teaspoon ground cumin
¾   cup (3 ounces) shredded reduced-fat Cheddar cheese
3   cups shredded iceberg lettuce
¼   cup plus 2 tablespoons nonfat sour cream

1. Cook turkey in a large nonstick skillet over medium heat until browned, stirring until it crumbles. Add 1 cup salsa, spinach, and cream cheese; cook until cheese melts, stirring often. Remove from skillet; set aside. Wipe skillet dry with a paper towel.

2. Place skillet over medium heat until hot. Coat both sides of tortillas with cooking spray. Place 1 tortilla in skillet. Cook 15 seconds on each side. Spoon about ⅓ cup turkey mixture across center of tortilla. Roll up; place, seam side down, in a 13- x 9- x 2-inch baking dish coated with cooking spray. Repeat procedure with remaining tortillas and turkey mixture.

3. Combine remaining 1 cup salsa, tomato, and cumin; pour over tortillas. Bake, uncovered, at 350° for 25 to 30 minutes or until mixture is thoroughly heated. Sprinkle enchiladas with cheese, and let stand 2 minutes.

4. Arrange lettuce evenly on individual serving plates. Place 2 enchiladas on each plate. Top each serving with 1 tablespoon sour cream. Yield: 6 servings.

Turkey Enchiladas

Pesto Pasta and Turkey

Time: Prep 15 minutes; Cook 12 minutes

Per Serving:
Calories 362
Carbohydrate 32.2g
Protein 36.2g
Fat 8.6g
Fiber 1.0g
Cholesterol 66mg
Sodium 320mg
Calcium 229mg
Exchanges:
2 Grain
4 Lean Meat

1	(7-ounce) jar roasted red peppers in water
¾	cup tightly packed fresh basil leaves
¼	cup tightly packed fresh cilantro leaves
¼	cup grated Parmesan cheese
3	tablespoons canned no-salt-added chicken broth
1	tablespoon olive oil
1	clove garlic, halved
1	tablespoon all-purpose flour
1	cup evaporated skimmed milk
¼	cup dry white wine
¼	teaspoon salt
10	ounces cavatappi (corkscrew pasta), uncooked
3	cups cubed cooked turkey breast
2	tablespoons pine nuts, toasted

1. Drain peppers, reserving liquid. Chop enough peppers to measure ¼ cup; set aside. Reserve remaining peppers in liquid for another use.

2. Position knife blade in food processor bowl; add basil and next 5 ingredients. Process 1 minute, scraping sides of processor bowl once; set aside.

3. Place flour in a medium saucepan. Gradually add milk, stirring until smooth. Add wine and salt. Cook over medium heat, stirring constantly, until mixture is slightly thickened. Stir in basil mixture.

4. Cook pasta according to package directions, omitting salt and fat; drain. Combine pasta and basil mixture in a serving bowl; toss gently. Add ¼ cup red pepper, turkey, and pine nuts; toss gently. Serve immediately. Yield: 8 (1-cup) servings.

Traditional pesto is high in fat. But in this recipe chicken broth replaces most of the olive oil, and the fat is trimmed considerably.

Tropical Cornish Hens

Time: Prep 18 minutes; Cook 1 hour

1¾	cups water
½	cup wild rice, uncooked
⅔	cup long-grain rice, uncooked
2	(1-pound) Cornish hens, skinned
2	tablespoons curry powder
	Vegetable cooking spray
½	cup peach sauce
¼	cup fresh lime juice
4	kiwifruit, peeled and cut into ¼-inch-thick slices
2	carambolas (star fruit), cut into ¼-inch-thick slices
1	ripe mango, peeled, seeded, and cut into 1-inch pieces

Per Serving:
Calories 480
Carbohydrate 64.5g
Protein 34.9g
Fat 9.0g
Fiber 7.8g
Cholesterol 91mg
Sodium 353mg
Calcium 63mg
Exchanges:
2 Grain
2 Fruit
3½ Lean Meat

1. Combine water and wild rice in a saucepan. Bring to a boil. Cover, reduce heat, and simmer 30 minutes. Stir in long-grain rice; cover and simmer 20 minutes or until rice is tender and liquid is absorbed. Set aside, and keep warm.

2. Meanwhile, remove and discard giblets from hens. Rinse hens under cold water; pat dry with paper towels. Split hens in half lengthwise, using an electric knife. Sprinkle with curry powder. Place hens, cut sides down, on a rack in a roasting pan coated with cooking spray. Bake, uncovered, at 350° for 30 minutes.

3. Combine peach sauce and lime juice. Combine 1 tablespoon peach sauce mixture, kiwifruit, carambola, and mango; toss well. Baste hens with remaining peach mixture. Bake 20 minutes, basting occasionally with peach mixture. Arrange kiwifruit mixture around hens. Bake 10 minutes or until hens are done and fruit is thoroughly heated. Serve hens and fruit mixture over rice. Yield: 4 servings.

Note: Grocery stores stock peach sauce either with the Asian foods or with the jellies in the condiments aisle of the store.

Tropical Cornish Hens

Grilled Mahimahi with Pineapple

Time: Prep 10 minutes; Marinate 2 hours; Cook 10 minutes

Per Serving:
Calories 248
Carbohydrate 32.1g
Protein 21.1g
Fat 3.9g
Fiber 2.4g
Cholesterol 80mg
Sodium 491mg
Calcium 28mg
Exchanges:
2 Fruit
3 Lean Meat

1½   cups unsweetened pineapple juice
¼   cup plus 2 tablespoons low-sodium soy sauce
3   tablespoons brown sugar
3   tablespoons minced green onions
1   tablespoon dark sesame oil
2   teaspoons peeled, minced gingerroot
1½   teaspoons minced garlic
½   teaspoon dried crushed red pepper
4   (4-ounce) mahimahi fillets
8   (½-inch-thick) slices fresh pineapple
     Vegetable cooking spray
     Fresh spinach leaves (optional)
     Green onion curls (optional)

1. Combine first 8 ingredients. Place fish and pineapple slices in a large shallow baking dish. Pour half of pineapple juice mixture over fish and pineapple. Cover and marinate in refrigerator 2 hours, turning fish and pineapple occasionally. Divide remaining pineapple juice mixture in half; set aside.

Grilled Mahimahi with Pineapple

2. Remove fish and pineapple from marinade; discard marinade.

3. Coat grill rack with cooking spray; place on grill over medium-hot coals (350° to 400°). Place fish and pineapple on rack; grill, covered, 5 to 6 minutes on each side or until fish flakes easily when tested with a fork and pineapple is tender, basting often with half of reserved pineapple juice mixture.

4. Pour remaining half of reserved pineapple juice mixture through a wire-mesh strainer into a small saucepan, discarding solids remaining in strainer. Bring to a boil over medium heat. Remove from heat. Transfer fish and pineapple to a serving platter. Drizzle with warm pineapple juice mixture. If desired, garnish with spinach leaves and green onion curls. Yield: 4 servings.

Poached Salmon with Yellow Tomato Salsa

Time: Prep 15 minutes; Chill 1 hour

½ cup water
⅓ cup dry white wine
1 tablespoon coarsely chopped onion
½ teaspoon freshly ground pepper
4 (4-ounce) salmon fillets
1 cup peeled, seeded, and chopped yellow tomato
½ cup plus 2 tablespoons peeled, seeded, and chopped
  cucumber
⅓ cup chopped sweet red pepper
¼ cup chopped green onions
2 tablespoons chopped fresh parsley
3 tablespoons lime juice
1 teaspoon minced garlic
½ teaspoon hot sauce
¼ teaspoon salt
  Fresh watercress sprigs (optional)
  Lemon wedges (optional)

1. Combine first 4 ingredients in a large nonstick skillet. Bring to a boil over medium heat. Reduce heat; add fish, skin sides down. Cover and simmer 5 to 7 minutes or until fish flakes easily when tested with a fork. Transfer fish and cooking liquid to a shallow baking dish. Cover and chill thoroughly.

2. Combine tomato and next 8 ingredients, stirring well. Cover and chill at least 1 hour.

3. Remove fish from liquid; discard liquid. Place fish on individual watercress-lined serving plates, if desired. Spoon tomato mixture over fish. Garnish with lemon wedges, if desired. Yield: 4 servings.

Per Serving:
Calories 209
Carbohydrate 6.0g
Protein 24.2g
Fat 9.6g
Fiber 1.3g
Cholesterol 74mg
Sodium 215mg
Calcium 23mg
Exchanges:
3 Medium-Fat Meat

Poached Salmon with Yellow Tomato Salsa

Tilapia in Corn Husks

Time: Prep 30 minutes; Cook 20 minutes

6   large ears fresh corn with husks
½   cup water
¼   cup chopped onion
1   tablespoon fresh lime juice
¼   teaspoon salt
¼   teaspoon ground cumin
¼   teaspoon pepper
1   (4½-ounce) can chopped green chiles, drained
1   (2-ounce) jar diced pimiento, drained
6   (4-ounce) tilapia or orange roughy fillets
    Vegetable cooking spray
    Lime wedges (optional)

1. Carefully peel back husks from corn, leaving husks attached to stem. Remove corn cobs; set aside. Remove and discard silks. Cut six 8-inch pieces of string. Place husks and string in a large bowl; add water to cover. Set aside.

Tilapia in Corn Husks

2. Cut enough corn from cobs to measure ¾ cup. Reserve remaining corn for another use. Combine corn and ½ cup water in a saucepan. Bring to a boil; cover, reduce heat, and simmer 10 minutes or until corn is tender; drain. Combine corn, onion, and next 6 ingredients, stirring well.

3. Drain husks and string; pat dry with paper towels. Place 1 fillet in each husk near the stem. Top each fillet with ¼ cup corn mixture. Return husks to original position, and tie tips with string.

4. Coat grill rack with cooking spray, and place on grill over medium-hot coals (350° to 400°). Place husk packets on rack; grill, covered, 10 minutes on each side or until fish flakes easily when tested with a fork. Remove string; place husk packets on serving plates. Garnish with lime wedges, if desired. Yield: 6 servings.

Note: To bake without corn husks, place fish in a 13- x 9- x 2-inch baking dish coated with cooking spray. Top with corn mixture. Bake, uncovered, at 350° for 15 minutes or until fish flakes easily when tested with a fork.

Swordfish with Mushroom-Tomato Sauce

Time: Prep 8 minutes; Cook 12 minutes

	Butter-flavored vegetable cooking spray
2	teaspoons reduced-calorie margarine
4	(4-ounce) swordfish steaks (¾ inch thick)
2	cups coarsely chopped fresh shiitake mushrooms
½	cup seeded, chopped tomato
¼	cup chopped green onions
¼	cup dry white wine
¼	cup clam juice
2	tablespoons no-salt-added tomato paste
2	teaspoons minced garlic
1	teaspoon minced fresh thyme
¼	teaspoon ground cumin
1	tablespoon lemon juice

Per Serving:
Calories 186
Carbohydrate 9.1g
Protein 23.9g
Fat 6.1g
Fiber 1.1g
Cholesterol 44mg
Sodium 161mg
Calcium 22mg
Exchanges:
1 Vegetable
3 Lean Meat

1. Coat a large nonstick skillet with cooking spray; add margarine. Place over medium heat until hot. Add fish, and cook 3 minutes on each side; set aside, and keep warm. Wipe skillet dry with a paper towel.

2. Coat skillet with cooking spray. Add mushrooms, and sauté 1 minute. Add tomato and next 7 ingredients, stirring well. Top with fish; cover and cook over medium heat 5 minutes or until fish flakes easily when tested with a fork. Transfer fish to a serving platter. Stir lemon juice into tomato mixture, and spoon over fish. Serve immediately. Yield: 4 servings.

Seasoned Crab Cakes with Lemon Sauce

Time: Prep 20 minutes; Cook 10 minutes

Per Serving:
Calories 227
Carbohydrate 20.7g
Protein 21.5g
Fat 6.0g
Fiber 0.8g
Cholesterol 86mg
Sodium 567mg
Calcium 154mg
Exchanges:
1 Grain
2½ Lean Meat

1½	cups soft breadcrumbs
2	tablespoons minced green onions
2	tablespoons minced sweet red pepper
2	tablespoons nonfat mayonnaise
1	tablespoon finely chopped fresh parsley
½	teaspoon dry mustard
¼	teaspoon ground red pepper
1	egg white
1	pound fresh crabmeat, drained
	Butter-flavored vegetable cooking spray
1	teaspoon vegetable oil
	Lemon Sauce

1. Combine first 8 ingredients; stir well. Add crabmeat, stirring gently. Shape into 5 patties.

2. Coat a large nonstick skillet with cooking spray; add oil. Place over medium heat until hot. Add patties; cook 5 minutes on each side or until golden. Serve with Lemon Sauce. Yield: 5 servings.

Lemon Sauce

	Vegetable cooking spray
1	tablespoon margarine
¼	cup finely chopped shallots
1	clove garlic, minced
½	cup canned no-salt-added chicken broth
¼	cup dry white wine
¼	teaspoon grated lemon rind
3	tablespoons fresh lemon juice
¼	teaspoon pepper
⅛	teaspoon salt
2	teaspoons cornstarch
3	tablespoons evaporated skimmed milk

1. Coat a small saucepan with cooking spray; add margarine. Place over medium-high heat until margarine melts. Add shallots and garlic; sauté until tender. Add chicken broth and next 5 ingredients; bring to a boil, stirring often.

2. Combine cornstarch and milk, stirring until smooth. Add to broth mixture, stirring constantly. Cook, stirring constantly, until mixture thickens. Yield: ¾ cup.

Lemon-Parsley Broiled Scallops

Time: Prep 10 minutes; Marinate 10 minutes; Cook 12 minutes

1   pound fresh sea scallops
1   teaspoon grated lemon rind
2   tablespoons fresh lemon juice
1   tablespoon olive oil
1   tablespoon water
2   teaspoons minced fresh parsley
½   teaspoon freshly ground pepper
2   cloves garlic, minced

Per Serving:
Calories 135
Carbohydrate 4.1g
Protein 19.2g
Fat 4.3g
Fiber 0.1g
Cholesterol 37mg
Sodium 183mg
Calcium 14mg
Exchanges:
3 Lean Meat

1. Place scallops in a shallow 2½-quart baking dish. Combine lemon rind and remaining 6 ingredients; stir well. Pour over scallops; cover and marinate in refrigerator 10 minutes.

2. Broil 5½ inches from heat (with electric oven door partially opened) 6 minutes; stir well. Broil 6 additional minutes or until scallops are done. Yield: 5 servings.

Note: These scallops are also delicious when grilled. To grill, place scallops on five 10-inch skewers. Grill, covered, over medium-hot coals (350° to 400°) 3 minutes on each side or until scallops are opaque.

Southwestern Grilled Shrimp

Time: Prep 30 minutes; Marinate 2 hours; Cook 6 minutes

Per Serving:
Calories 138
Carbohydrate 3.7g
Protein 19.9g
Fat 4.6g
Fiber 0.6g
Cholesterol 180mg
Sodium 379mg
Calcium 42mg
Exchanges:
2½ Lean Meat

1½ pounds unpeeled large fresh shrimp
2 tablespoons fresh lime juice, divided
1 tablespoon water
1 tablespoon low-sodium soy sauce
1 teaspoon minced garlic
1 teaspoon olive oil
1 jalapeño pepper, seeded and halved
3 tomatillos, husked
¼ cup plus 2 tablespoons cubed avocado
¼ teaspoon sugar
⅛ teaspoon salt
⅛ teaspoon freshly ground pepper
Vegetable cooking spray

1. Peel and devein shrimp; place in a large heavy-duty, zip-top plastic bag. Combine 1 tablespoon lime juice and next 4 ingredients, and pour over shrimp. Seal bag; shake gently. Marinate in refrigerator 2 hours.

Southwestern Grilled Shrimp

2. Place jalapeño pepper halves, skin sides up, on a baking sheet, and flatten with palm of hand. Broil 5½ inches from heat (with electric oven door partially opened) 10 minutes or until charred. Place in ice water until cool. Remove from water; peel and discard skin.

3. Place jalapeño pepper and tomatillos in container of an electric blender; cover and process until chopped. Add remaining 1 tablespoon lime juice, avocado, and next 3 ingredients; cover and process until smooth. Chill.

4. Remove shrimp from marinade; discard marinade. Thread shrimp onto four 8-inch skewers. Coat grill rack with cooking spray; place on grill over medium-hot coals (350° to 400°). Place shrimp on rack; grill, covered, 3 to 4 minutes on each side or until done. Remove shrimp from skewers, and place on serving plates. Serve with tomatillo mixture. Yield: 4 servings.

Salads & Dressings

Wilted Greens with Warm Bacon Dressing (page 172)

Festive Cranberry-Pear Salad

Time: Prep 8 minutes; Cook 6 minutes

Per Serving:
Calories 99
Carbohydrate 22.0g
Protein 0.9g
Fat 1.6g
Fiber 1.9g
Cholesterol 0mg
Sodium 11mg
Calcium 13mg
Exchanges:
1½ Fruit

1¼	cups fresh cranberries
⅓	cup sugar
⅓	cup water
2	cups cubed fresh pear
½	cup diced celery
2	tablespoons minced walnuts
¼	teaspoon ground nutmeg
	Dash of ground allspice
	Lettuce leaves (optional)

1. Combine first 3 ingredients in a small saucepan; bring to a boil. Cook over medium-high heat 6 minutes or until cranberries pop, stirring often. Remove from heat, and cool completely.

2. Combine cranberry mixture, pear, and next 4 ingredients in a medium bowl; stir gently. Serve salad on lettuce leaves, if desired. Yield: 6 servings.

Citrus-Jicama Salad

Time: Prep 13 minutes; Chill 30 minutes

Per Serving:
Calories 78
Carbohydrate 19.2g
Protein 1.6g
Fat 0.2g
Fiber 5.6g
Cholesterol 0mg
Sodium 2mg
Calcium 58mg
Exchange:
1 Fruit

5	large oranges, peeled and cut crosswise into ¼-inch-thick slices
⅔	cup peeled, diced jicama
¼	cup sliced green onions
½	cup unsweetened orange juice
2	tablespoons chopped fresh cilantro
2	tablespoons lime juice
½	teaspoon sugar
⅛	teaspoon ground red pepper

1. Combine first 3 ingredients. Combine orange juice and remaining 4 ingredients; pour over orange mixture, and toss gently. Cover and chill at least 30 minutes. Serve with a slotted spoon. Yield: 6 (¾-cup) servings.

Orange and Onion Salad

Time: Prep 9 minutes; Chill 30 minutes

2 tablespoons rice wine vinegar
2 tablespoons low-sodium soy sauce
2 teaspoons dark sesame oil
¼ teaspoon grated orange rind
2 large oranges, peeled, seeded, and sliced
1 small purple onion, thinly sliced
3 cups torn red leaf lettuce

Per Serving:
Calories 42
Carbohydrate 6.1g
Protein 0.7g
Fat 1.6g
Fiber 2.1g
Cholesterol 0mg
Sodium 132mg
Calcium 29mg
Exchange:
1 Vegetable

1. Combine first 4 ingredients in a small bowl, stirring with a wire whisk. Arrange orange and onion in a 13- x 9- x 2-inch dish. Pour vinegar mixture over orange and onion. Cover and chill at least 30 minutes.

2. Arrange lettuce evenly on individual salad plates. Spoon orange and onion over lettuce, using a slotted spoon. Drizzle vinegar mixture over salads. Yield: 6 servings.

I enjoy the intense nutty flavor that dark sesame oil adds. A little goes a long way.

Mixed Greens with Balsamic Vinaigrette

Time: Prep 10 minutes; Chill 30 minutes

Per Serving:
Calories 43
Carbohydrate 4.0g
Protein 0.9g
Fat 2.7g
Fiber 0.6g
Cholesterol 0mg
Sodium 95mg
Calcium 14mg
Exchanges:
1 Vegetable
1 Fat

½ cup canned no-salt-added chicken broth, undiluted
¼ cup balsamic vinegar
1½ tablespoons olive oil
1 tablespoon honey
2 teaspoons coarse-grained mustard
¼ teaspoon salt
1 large clove garlic, minced
1 (6-ounce) package mixed salad greens
7 cups torn Bibb lettuce (2 large heads)
½ teaspoon freshly ground pepper

1. Combine first 7 ingredients. Cover and chill at least 30 minutes.

2. Combine mixed greens and Bibb lettuce in a large bowl. Add vinegar mixture, and toss. Arrange evenly on individual salad plates, and sprinkle with pepper. Yield: 8 (1½-cup) servings.

Pineapple Slaw

Time: Prep 10 minutes; Chill 30 minutes

Per Serving:
Calories 81
Carbohydrate 14.0g
Protein 1.8g
Fat 2.8g
Fiber 2.1g
Cholesterol 0mg
Sodium 4mg
Calcium 31mg
Exchanges:
1 Vegetable
½ Fruit
1 Fat

1 (8-ounce) carton pineapple or vanilla low-fat yogurt
3 tablespoons reduced-calorie mayonnaise
½ teaspoon lemon juice
5 cups thinly sliced green cabbage
1 (8-ounce) can pineapple tidbits in juice, drained

1. Stir yogurt; spoon onto several layers of heavy-duty paper towels, and spread to ½-inch thickness. Cover with paper towels; let stand 5 minutes. Scrape into a bowl, using a rubber spatula; stir in mayonnaise and lemon juice.

2. Combine cabbage and pineapple in a bowl; toss mixture well. Add yogurt mixture, tossing gently to coat. Cover and chill. Yield: 4 (1-cup) servings.

Pineapple Slaw

Romaine and Strawberry Salad

Romaine and Strawberry Salad

Time: Prep 7 minutes

2	cups torn romaine lettuce
½	cup halved fresh strawberries
1	tablespoon coarsely chopped purple onion
1	tablespoon slivered almonds, toasted
1	tablespoon honey
1	tablespoon balsamic vinegar

1. Combine first 4 ingredients in a bowl; toss gently.

2. Combine honey and vinegar, stirring well. Drizzle over salad, and toss gently. Yield: 2 servings.

Per Serving:
Calories 119
Carbohydrate 19.1g
Protein 3.6g
Fat 3.8g
Fiber 2.3g
Cholesterol 6mg
Sodium 130mg
Calcium 125mg
Exchanges:
1 Vegetable
1 Fruit
1 Fat

Wilted Greens with Warm Bacon Dressing

Time: Prep 5 minutes; Cook 13 minutes

Per Serving:
Calories 56
Carbohydrate 5.1g
Protein 4.0g
Fat 2.6g
Fiber 1.1g
Cholesterol 10mg
Sodium 195mg
Calcium 14mg
Exchanges:
1 Vegetable
1 Fat

2	cups water
½	cup English peas
6	cups gourmet salad greens (about ¼ pound)
½	cup thinly sliced green onions
4	slices turkey bacon, diced
¼	cup water
2	tablespoons red wine vinegar
2	tablespoons fresh lemon juice
	Coarsely ground pepper (optional)

1. Bring 2 cups water to a boil in a saucepan; add peas. Cover and cook 7 minutes or until crisp-tender. Drain and rinse under cold running water; drain well.

2. Combine peas, salad greens, and green onions in a large serving bowl.

3. Cook turkey bacon in a nonstick skillet over medium heat 4 minutes or until crisp. Add ¼ cup water, vinegar, and lemon juice to skillet; cook 2 minutes. Immediately pour warm dressing over salad, and toss gently to coat. Sprinkle salad with pepper, if desired. Yield: 4 (1½-cup) servings.

Lentil Salad

Time: Prep 5 minutes; Cook 20 minutes

Per Serving:
Calories 309
Carbohydrate 40.5g
Protein 19.8g
Fat 8.9g
Fiber 8.2g
Cholesterol 13mg
Sodium 326mg
Calcium 118mg
Exchanges:
2½ Grain
1 Vegetable
1 Medium-Fat Meat

1¼	cups dried lentils
3	tablespoons lemon juice
1½	tablespoons olive oil
½	teaspoon dried thyme
¼	teaspoon salt
⅛	teaspoon coarsely ground pepper
1	clove garlic, crushed
1½	cups quartered cherry tomatoes
1	cup diced cucumber
½	cup crumbled feta cheese
⅓	cup thinly sliced celery
	Romaine lettuce leaves (optional)

Lentil Salad

1. Place lentils in a large saucepan; add water to cover 2 inches above lentils, and bring to a boil. Cover, reduce heat, and simmer 20 minutes or until tender. Drain well.

2. Combine lemon juice and next 5 ingredients in a bowl; stir with a wire whisk until blended. Add lentils, tomatoes, and next 3 ingredients; toss gently to coat. Serve on lettuce-lined plates, if desired. Yield: 4 (1½-cup) servings.

Southwestern Tabbouleh

Time: Prep 7 minutes; Stand 1 hour; Chill 4 hours

Per Serving:
Calories 171
Carbohydrate 29.7g
Protein 5.1g
Fat 3.3g
Fiber 2.1g
Cholesterol 0mg
Sodium 242mg
Calcium 24mg
Exchanges:
1½ Grain
1 Fat

1	cup bulgur (cracked wheat), uncooked
2	cups boiling water
3	tablespoons low-sodium soy sauce
2	tablespoons lemon juice
1	tablespoon olive oil
1	cup seeded, diced tomato
1	cup peeled, minced jicama
½	cup minced fresh cilantro
3	tablespoons minced fresh chives
2	tablespoons minced fresh mint
1	tablespoon peeled, grated gingerroot
2	teaspoons minced garlic

1. Combine bulgur and water in a large bowl; let stand 1 hour or until bulgur is tender and liquid is absorbed. Combine soy sauce, lemon juice, and oil, stirring well. Add to bulgur; toss well. Add tomato and remaining ingredients; toss. Cover and chill at least 4 hours. Yield: 5 (1-cup) servings.

Potato Salad with Asparagus

Time: Prep 6 minutes; Cook 20 minutes; Chill 1 hour

Per Serving:
Calories 98
Carbohydrate 16.4g
Protein 2.9g
Fat 2.5g
Fiber 2.5g
Cholesterol 0mg
Sodium 82mg
Calcium 22mg
Exchange:
1 Grain

4	medium-size round red potatoes (about ¾ pound)
½	pound fresh asparagus spears (about 10 spears)
2	tablespoons sliced green onions
¼	cup white wine vinegar
2	teaspoons olive oil
1	teaspoon Dijon mustard
	Dash of salt
	Dash of ground white pepper
4	Bibb lettuce leaves

1. Wash potatoes. Cook in boiling water to cover 20 to 25 minutes or until tender; drain and cool slightly. Cut each potato into 6 wedges. Set aside.

2. Meanwhile, snap off tough ends of asparagus, and remove scales from spears with a knife or vegetable peeler, if desired. Cut asparagus into 1-inch pieces. Arrange asparagus in a vegetable steamer over boiling water. Cover and steam 4 to 5 minutes or until crisp-tender. Rinse with cold water.

3. Combine potato, asparagus, and green onions in a shallow dish. Combine vinegar and next 4 ingredients. Pour vinegar mixture over potato mixture, and toss gently. Cover and chill at least 1 hour, stirring occasionally. Spoon salad evenly onto four lettuce-lined salad plates. Yield: 4 servings.

Potato Salad with Asparagus

Barley and Corn Salad

Barley and Corn Salad

Time: Prep 8 minutes; Cook 40 minutes

Per Serving:
Calories 196
Carbohydrate 34.8g
Protein 4.7g
Fat 5.4g
Fiber 6.8g
Cholesterol 0mg
Sodium 205mg
Calcium 19mg
Exchanges:
1½ Grain
1 Vegetable
1 Fat

3	cups water
1	cup pearl barley, uncooked
¼	cup fresh lime juice
1	tablespoon seeded, minced jalapeño pepper
2	tablespoons vegetable oil
½	teaspoon salt
⅛	teaspoon pepper
1	cup corn, cut from cob (about 2 large ears)
½	cup peeled, seeded, and diced cucumber
½	cup diced tomato
½	cup diced green pepper
½	cup chopped purple onion

1. Bring water to a boil in a medium saucepan; gradually stir in barley. Cover, reduce heat, and simmer 40 minutes or until barley is tender and water is absorbed. Let cool.

2. Combine lime juice and next 4 ingredients, stirring with a wire whisk. Combine barley, corn, and remaining 4 ingredients in a large bowl; add lime juice mixture to barley mixture, tossing to coat. Yield: 6 (1-cup) servings.

Confetti Pasta Salad

Time: Prep 10 minutes; Cook 8 minutes; Chill 30 minutes

¾	cup commercial low-fat Ranch-style dressing
½	cup plain nonfat yogurt
1	teaspoon chopped fresh dillweed
2	cups small seashell macaroni, uncooked
1½	cups frozen English peas, thawed
½	cup diced sweet yellow pepper
½	cup diced sweet red pepper
¾	cup (3 ounces) cubed reduced-fat sharp Cheddar cheese
	Dillweed sprigs (optional)

Per Serving:
Calories 204
Carbohydrate 28.6g
Protein 9.9g
Fat 5.4g
Fiber 2.5g
Cholesterol 10mg
Sodium 440mg
Calcium 178mg
Exchanges:
1½ Grain
1 Vegetable
1 Fat

1. Combine first 3 ingredients in a large bowl; stir mixture well.

2. Cook macaroni in boiling water 6 minutes. Add peas, and cook 2 additional minutes; drain well. Add macaroni mixture, peppers, and cheese to dressing mixture, tossing to coat. Cover salad, and chill at least 30 minutes. Garnish with dillweed sprigs, if desired. Yield: 6 (1-cup) servings.

Note: You can substitute elbow macaroni for seashell, if desired.

Confetti Pasta Salad

Mexican Beef Salad

Time: Prep 15 minutes; Marinate 30 minutes; Cook 10 minutes

Per Serving:
Calories 375
Carbohydrate 37.6g
Protein 26.5g
Fat 13.4g
Fiber 4.3g
Cholesterol 62mg
Sodium 341mg
Calcium 133mg
Exchanges:
1 Grain
1 Vegetable
3 Medium-Fat Meat

1	pound lean boneless top round steak
1	tablespoon chili powder
½	teaspoon onion powder
½	teaspoon ground oregano
½	teaspoon ground cumin
¼	teaspoon garlic powder
¼	teaspoon ground red pepper
2	teaspoons vegetable oil
1	(8-ounce) carton low-fat sour cream
2	tablespoons canned chopped green chiles
1	teaspoon chili powder
¼	teaspoon ground cumin
⅛	teaspoon garlic powder
6	(10-inch) flour tortillas
	Vegetable cooking spray
6	cups shredded iceberg lettuce
1	cup fresh cilantro sprigs
1	cup chopped tomato
¾	cup canned kidney beans, drained
¾	cup frozen whole-kernel corn, thawed
	Jalapeño pepper slices (optional)
	Additional cilantro sprigs (optional)

1. Trim fat from steak. Combine 1 tablespoon chili powder and next 6 ingredients in a small bowl. Rub spice mixture evenly over both sides of steak. Cover steak, and marinate in refrigerator 30 minutes.

2. Meanwhile, combine sour cream and next 4 ingredients in a small bowl. Cover and chill.

3. Press 1 tortilla gently into a medium bowl. Microwave at HIGH 1½ minutes or until tortilla is crisp. Repeat procedure with remaining tortillas.

4. Place steak on rack of a broiler pan coated with cooking spray. Broil 5½ inches from heat (with electric oven door partially opened) 5 minutes on each side or to desired degree of doneness. Cut steak diagonally across grain into thin strips.

Mexican Beef Salad

5. Combine lettuce and 1 cup cilantro; place evenly into tortilla bowls. Arrange tomato, beans, corn, and steak over lettuce mixture. Dollop with sour cream mixture. Garnish with jalapeño slices and additional cilantro sprigs, if desired. Yield: 6 servings.

Savory Chicken and Peach Salad

Time: Prep 15 minutes

Per Serving:
Calories 265
Carbohydrate 21.4g
Protein 31.9g
Fat 6.0g
Fiber 3.1g
Cholesterol 72mg
Sodium 449mg
Calcium 36mg
Exchanges:
1 Vegetable
1 Fruit
3 Lean Meat

¼	cup plus 2 tablespoons nonfat mayonnaise
¼	cup plus 2 tablespoons nonfat sour cream
¾	teaspoon sugar
¾	teaspoon lemon juice
½	teaspoon curry powder
⅛	teaspoon salt
⅛	teaspoon ground ginger
⅛	teaspoon ground cinnamon
8	cups torn Bibb lettuce
2	cups cubed cooked chicken breast (about 12 ounces cooked)
2	cups peeled, sliced peach (about 1¼ pounds)
16	Bibb lettuce leaves
2	tablespoons pine nuts, toasted

1. Combine first 8 ingredients in a large bowl; stir well. Add torn lettuce, chicken, and peach; toss gently.

2. Spoon 2 cups salad onto each of four lettuce-lined plates, and sprinkle pine nuts over each serving. Yield: 4 servings.

Step 1

Step 2

Step 3

*Nothing is as summery as a ripe fresh peach. My preference is to eat them whole, peach fuzz and all. But to peel them for a recipe, you can use a paring knife or a vegetable peeler, or you can slip the skins off by blanching them. To blanch them, follow these steps. **Step 1:** Drop peaches into a pot of boiling water for 30 seconds to 1 minute, depending on the ripeness of the fruit. **Step 2:** Immediately immerse them in cold water. **Step 3:** Peel the skins; they should come right off.*

Chinese Chicken Salad

Time: Prep 7 minutes; Cook 15 minutes

2	(4-ounce) skinned, boned chicken breast halves
1	(10-ounce) package frozen broccoli flowerets, thawed
½	cup sliced water chestnuts, drained
½	cup mandarin oranges in light syrup, drained
1	teaspoon grated orange rind
⅓	cup unsweetened orange juice
3	tablespoons cider vinegar
1	tablespoon low-sodium soy sauce
2	teaspoons granulated sugar substitute
1½	teaspoons dark sesame oil
¼	teaspoon salt
¼	teaspoon ground ginger
⅛	teaspoon dried crushed red pepper
4	cups shredded Chinese cabbage
2	tablespoons chow mein noodles
1	tablespoon sesame seeds, toasted

Per Serving:
Calories 194
Carbohydrate 16.3g
Protein 21.5g
Fat 5.2g
Fiber 2.4g
Cholesterol 48mg
Sodium 346mg
Calcium 131mg
Exchanges:
1 Fruit
3 Very Lean Meat

1. Place chicken in a non-stick skillet; add water to cover. Bring to a boil; cover, reduce heat, and simmer 15 minutes or until tender. Drain; cut chicken into strips.

2. Combine chicken strips, broccoli, water chestnuts, and oranges. Combine orange rind and next 8 ingredients. Pour juice mixture over chicken mixture; toss lightly.

3. To serve, arrange 1 cup cabbage on each of four serving plates, and top evenly with chicken mixture. Sprinkle evenly with noodles and sesame seeds. Yield: 4 servings.

Chinese Chicken Salad

Salad Niçoise

Salad Niçoise

Time: Prep 9 minutes; Cook 26 minutes; Chill 2 hours

Per Serving:
Calories 234
Carbohydrate 17.9g
Protein 23.4g
Fat 7.5g
Fiber 4.2g
Cholesterol 33mg
Sodium 211mg
Calcium 64mg
Exchanges:
1 Grain
3 Lean Meat

3 tablespoons white wine vinegar
2 tablespoons water
1½ teaspoons Dijon mustard
½ teaspoon olive oil
⅛ teaspoon freshly ground pepper
2 small round red potatoes (about ¼ pound)
¼ pound green beans
2 tablespoons julienne-sliced sweet red pepper
1 tablespoon chopped purple onion
1 (6-ounce) tuna steak (¾ inch thick)
½ teaspoon olive oil
   Vegetable cooking spray
2 cups torn fresh spinach
4 cherry tomatoes, quartered
1 tablespoon sliced ripe olives

1. Combine first 5 ingredients in a small jar; cover tightly, and shake vigorously. Set aside.

2. Wash potatoes. Cook in boiling water to cover 20 minutes or just until tender. Drain; cool slightly. Cut into ¼-inch-thick slices.

3. Meanwhile, wash beans; trim ends, and remove strings. Arrange beans in a vegetable steamer over boiling water. Cover and steam 5 minutes or until crisp-tender. Drain.

4. Combine potato, green beans, red pepper, and onion; toss gently. Add half of vinegar mixture to potato mixture; toss gently. Cover and chill 2 hours.

5. Brush fish with ½ teaspoon olive oil. Place on rack of a broiler pan coated with cooking spray. Broil 5½ inches from heat (with electric oven door partially opened) 3 to 4 minutes on each side or until fish flakes easily when tested with a fork. Flake fish into pieces.

6. Place spinach on a serving platter. Arrange green bean mixture, fish, tomatoes, and olives over spinach. Drizzle remaining half of vinegar mixture over salad. Yield: 2 servings.

Curried Shrimp Salad

Time: Prep 18 minutes; Chill 30 minutes

Per Serving:
Calories 105
Carbohydrate 6.8g
Protein 16.9g
Fat 0.9g
Fiber 0.6g
Cholesterol 148mg
Sodium 369mg
Calcium 62mg
Exchanges:
1 Vegetable
2 Very Lean Meat

1½   quarts water
2   pounds uncooked medium shrimp
½   cup chopped celery
½   cup chopped green onions
1   (8-ounce) can sliced water chestnuts, drained
¼   cup plain nonfat yogurt
¼   cup nonfat mayonnaise
1   teaspoon curry powder
2   teaspoons reduced-sodium soy sauce
1   teaspoon lemon juice
¼   teaspoon pepper
     Bibb lettuce leaves (optional)

1. Bring 1½ quarts water to a boil; add shrimp, and reduce heat. Cook 3 minutes. Drain well, and rinse with cold water. Let shrimp cool; peel and devein.

2. Combine cooked shrimp, celery, green onions, and water chestnuts in a bowl; toss well. Combine yogurt and next 5 ingredients, stirring well. Add to shrimp mixture, tossing lightly to coat. Cover and chill at least 30 minutes. Serve on lettuce-lined plates, if desired. Yield: 6 servings.

Side Dishes

Jicama, Corn, and Green Pepper Skillet (page 197)

Broccoli-Rice Casserole

Broccoli-Rice Casserole

Time: Prep 10 minutes; Cook 25 minutes

Per Serving:
Calories 136
Carbohydrate 20.7g
Protein 7.8g
Fat 2.4g
Fiber 1.4g
Cholesterol 3mg
Sodium 308mg
Calcium 170mg
Exchanges:
1 Grain
1 Vegetable

3 cups chopped fresh broccoli
2 tablespoons reduced-calorie margarine, divided
¼ cup chopped onion
3 tablespoons all-purpose flour
½ teaspoon dry mustard
1¼ cups skim milk
⅛ teaspoon pepper
1¾ cups cooked long-grain rice (cooked without salt or fat)
1 cup (4 ounces) shredded fat-free Cheddar cheese
¼ cup nonfat mayonnaise
Vegetable cooking spray
⅓ cup crushed Melba toast

1. Cook broccoli in boiling water 3 minutes or until crisp-tender. Drain; plunge into cold water. Drain again, and set aside.

2. Melt 1½ tablespoons margarine in a saucepan; add onion, and sauté until tender. Add flour and mustard; cook, stirring constantly with a wire whisk, 1 minute. Gradually add milk to flour mixture, stirring constantly. Cook, stirring constantly, 2 minutes or until thickened and bubbly. Remove from heat; stir in pepper. Combine broccoli, milk mixture, rice, cheese, and mayonnaise. Spoon into a shallow 2-quart casserole coated with cooking spray.

3. Melt remaining 1½ teaspoons margarine; add toast crumbs. Sprinkle over broccoli mixture. Bake at 350° for 25 minutes or until heated. Yield: 8 (½-cup) servings.

Polenta with Sun-Dried Tomatoes

Time: Prep 17 minutes; Cook 6 minutes

1	cup sun-dried tomatoes (packed without oil)
1	cup hot water
	Olive oil-flavored vegetable cooking spray
1	teaspoon olive oil
½	cup finely chopped shallots
2	cloves garlic, crushed
2	(14¼-ounce) cans no-salt-added chicken broth
1½	cups water
½	teaspoon salt
½	teaspoon cracked pepper
1⅓	cups instant polenta, uncooked
½	cup grated Asiago or Parmesan cheese

Per Serving:
Calories 100
Carbohydrate 16.7g
Protein 3.7g
Fat 1.9g
Fiber 0.9g
Cholesterol 3mg
Sodium 279mg
Calcium 56mg
Exchange:
1 Grain

1. Combine tomatoes and hot water in a small bowl. Cover and let stand 15 minutes; drain. Coarsely chop tomatoes; set aside.

2. Meanwhile, coat a large saucepan with cooking spray; add oil. Place over medium-high heat until hot. Add shallots and garlic; sauté until tender.

3. Add chicken broth and next 3 ingredients to saucepan; bring to a boil. Add polenta in a slow, steady stream, stirring constantly. Reduce heat to medium, and cook, stirring constantly, 3 to 5 minutes or until thickened. Remove from heat. Stir in tomato and cheese. Serve warm. Yield: 11 (½-cup) servings.

I like to serve this soft polenta instead of mashed potatoes as a side dish.

Vegetable-Barley Casserole

Time: Prep 10 minutes; Cook 45 minutes

Per Serving:
Calories 89
Carbohydrate 17.5g
Protein 2.6g
Fat 1.4g
Fiber 3.6g
Cholesterol 0mg
Sodium 238mg
Calcium 14mg
Exchange:
1 Grain

1	tablespoon reduced-calorie margarine
1½	cups sliced fresh mushrooms
¾	cup pearl barley, uncooked
⅓	cup chopped onion
2	tablespoons chopped fresh parsley
1	cup thinly sliced zucchini, halved
½	cup shredded carrot
1	(14½-ounce) can vegetable broth
½	teaspoon pepper

1. Melt margarine in a nonstick skillet over medium-high heat. Add mushrooms and next 3 ingredients; sauté 5 minutes or until barley is lightly browned. Place barley mixture, zucchini, and carrot in a 1½-quart baking dish.

2. Bring broth to a boil in a saucepan; pour broth over barley mixture, stirring gently. Stir in pepper. Cover and bake at 350° for 45 minutes or until barley is tender and liquid is absorbed. Yield: 8 servings.

Note: If desired, you may substitute 1 (14½-ounce) can chicken broth for the vegetable broth.

Pasta with Roasted Vegetables

Time: Prep 12 minutes; Cook 25 minutes

  1 large zucchini
  1 large yellow squash
  1 large sweet red pepper, seeded
  1 (8-ounce) package fresh mushrooms
  1 large onion, cut into thin wedges
  2 tablespoons balsamic vinegar
  2 teaspoons olive oil
  ½ teaspoon dried rosemary
  ½ teaspoon sugar
  ¼ teaspoon salt
  ¼ teaspoon freshly ground pepper
  2 large tomatoes, coarsely chopped
 10 ounces gemelli pasta, uncooked
  2 ounces crumbled goat cheese
  ¼ cup shredded fresh basil
     Freshly ground pepper (optional)

Per Serving:
Calories 160
Carbohydrate 28.3g
Protein 6.1g
Fat 2.9g
Fiber 2.4g
Cholesterol 5mg
Sodium 130mg
Calcium 51mg
Exchanges:
1½ Grain
1 Fat

1. Line a 15- x 10- x 1-inch jellyroll pan with aluminum foil. Cut zucchini, squash, and red pepper into 1-inch pieces. Place on prepared pan; add mushrooms and onion.

2. Combine vinegar and next 5 ingredients in a small bowl, stirring well. Brush over vegetables. Bake at 425° for 15 minutes. Stir vegetables, and add tomato. Bake 10 additional minutes or until vegetables are tender and golden.

3. Meanwhile, cook pasta according to package directions, omitting salt and fat; drain. Place pasta in a serving bowl. Add roasted vegetables; toss well. Top with goat cheese and basil. Sprinkle with freshly ground pepper, if desired. Yield: 10 (1-cup) servings.

Gemelli, a rope-shaped pasta, adds a special twist to this dish. If it's not available, you can substitute fusilli.

Mostaccioli with Eggplant Sauce

Time: Prep 10 minutes; Cook 12 minutes

¼ cup crumbled feta cheese
1 tablespoon chopped fresh basil
2 teaspoons red wine vinegar
Olive oil-flavored vegetable cooking spray
2 tablespoons chopped onion
1½ teaspoons minced garlic
1 cup peeled, cubed eggplant
½ cup peeled, seeded, and chopped tomato
½ cup canned no-salt-added chicken broth
¼ cup no-salt-added tomato sauce
⅛ teaspoon dried thyme
⅛ teaspoon salt
⅛ teaspoon pepper
2 ounces thin mostaccioli pasta, uncooked

1. Combine first 3 ingredients in a small bowl; set aside.

2. Coat a small nonstick skillet with cooking spray; place over medium-high heat until hot. Add onion and garlic; sauté 2 minutes or until tender. Add eggplant and next 6 ingredients; cook, uncovered, over medium heat 10 minutes, stirring often. Remove from heat, and keep warm.

3. Meanwhile, cook pasta according to package directions, omitting salt and fat; drain. Place pasta in a serving bowl. Add eggplant mixture and cheese mixture; toss gently. Yield: 2 servings.

Creamy Herbed Pasta

Time: Prep 15 minutes; Cook 10 minutes

1	tablespoon chopped sun-dried tomatoes (packed without oil)
1	tablespoon hot water
1	tablespoon chopped fresh basil
2	tablespoons Neufchâtel cheese, softened
2	tablespoons canned low-sodium chicken broth
1	teaspoon chopped fresh oregano
1	teaspoon minced garlic
1	teaspoon lemon juice
1/8	teaspoon dried crushed red pepper
4	ounces orecchiette pasta, uncooked

Per Serving:
Calories 129
Carbohydrate 21.7g
Protein 4.5g
Fat 2.3g
Fiber 0.1g
Cholesterol 6mg
Sodium 50mg
Calcium 11mg
Exchanges:
1½ Grain

1. Combine tomato and water in a small bowl; cover and let stand 15 minutes. Drain well, and set aside.

2. Combine basil and next 6 ingredients, stirring well.

3. Meanwhile, cook pasta according to package directions, omitting salt and fat; drain. Place pasta in a serving bowl. Add chopped tomato and cheese mixture; toss gently. Serve immediately. Yield: 4 (½-cup) servings.

Pasta Primavera with Mustard Sauce

Pasta Primavera with Mustard Sauce

Time: Prep 8 minutes; Cook 8 minutes

Per Serving:
Calories 158
Carbohydrate 26.2g
Protein 6.2g
Fat 3.3g
Fiber 2.3g
Cholesterol 2mg
Sodium 173mg
Calcium 64mg
Exchanges:
1½ Grain
1 Vegetable
1 Fat

1	tablespoon olive oil
⅓	cup minced shallots
2	cloves garlic, minced
¾	cup chopped tomato
2	tablespoons chopped fresh parsley
2	tablespoons country-style Dijon mustard
1	tablespoon balsamic vinegar
¼	teaspoon pepper
8	ounces linguine, uncooked
2	cups small cauliflower flowerets
2	cups small broccoli flowerets
¼	cup grated Parmesan cheese

1. Heat oil in a small saucepan over medium heat. Add shallots and garlic; sauté 2 minutes. Add tomato and next 4 ingredients; cook 3 minutes or until thoroughly heated. Set aside, and keep warm.

2. Meanwhile, cook pasta in boiling water 5 minutes, omitting salt and fat. Add cauliflower and broccoli; cook 3 additional minutes or until tender. Drain well. Combine pasta mixture and tomato mixture; toss well. Sprinkle with cheese. Yield: 8 (1-cup) servings.

Artichokes and Portabella Mushrooms

Time: Prep 6 minutes; Cook 13 minutes

1	cup chopped onion
½	cup minced fresh parsley
1	tablespoon no-salt-added tomato paste
1	teaspoon sugar
1	teaspoon dried basil
½	teaspoon dried thyme
¼	teaspoon salt
⅛	teaspoon pepper
2	cloves garlic, minced
1	(14½-ounce) can no-salt-added whole tomatoes, undrained and finely chopped
1	(9-ounce) package frozen artichoke hearts, thawed and halved
1	(6-ounce) package sliced fresh portabella mushrooms
1	tablespoon all-purpose flour
¼	cup dry white wine
¼	cup sliced pimiento-stuffed olives

Per Serving:
Calories 63
Carbohydrate 13.0g
Protein 3.0g
Fat 0.8g
Fiber 1.5g
Cholesterol 0mg
Sodium 183mg
Calcium 55mg
Exchanges:
2 Vegetable

1. Combine first 12 ingredients in a large skillet, stirring well. Bring to a boil; cover, reduce heat to medium, and cook 10 minutes or until artichoke halves are tender, stirring once.

2. Combine flour and wine, stirring until smooth. Add wine mixture and olives to vegetable mixture; cook, stirring constantly, until thickened. Yield: 6 servings.

Asparagus with Blue Cheese and Almonds

Time: Prep 7 minutes; Cook 6 minutes

Per Serving:
Calories 44
Carbohydrate 5.3g
Protein 3.1g
Fat 1.7g
Fiber 2.1g
Cholesterol 2mg
Sodium 37mg
Calcium 36mg
Exchange:
1 Vegetable

1½	pounds fresh asparagus spears
¾	cup canned no-salt-added chicken broth
¼	cup sliced green onions
1	teaspoon dried tarragon
12	Bibb lettuce leaves
2	tablespoons crumbled blue cheese
1½	tablespoons sliced almonds, toasted

1. Snap off tough ends of asparagus. Remove scales from stalks with a knife or vegetable peeler, if desired.

2. Place broth in a large skillet. Bring to a boil over medium-high heat. Add asparagus, green onions, and tarragon. Reduce heat, and simmer, uncovered, 6 to 8 minutes or until asparagus is crisp-tender. Remove asparagus from skillet, using a slotted spoon; discard broth remaining in skillet.

3. Arrange asparagus on lettuce leaves. Sprinkle with blue cheese and almonds. Yield: 6 servings.

Sesame Broccoli

Time: Prep 7 minutes; Cook 8 minutes

Per Serving:
Calories 73
Carbohydrate 8.7g
Protein 3.4g
Fat 3.4g
Fiber 3.3g
Cholesterol 0mg
Sodium 257mg
Calcium 66mg
Exchanges:
1 Vegetable
1 Fat

2	tablespoons plus 1 teaspoon low-sodium soy sauce
1	tablespoon rice wine vinegar
2¼	teaspoons sugar
2	teaspoons sesame oil
¾	teaspoon dried crushed red pepper
2	small cloves garlic, minced
6	cups broccoli flowerets
2	teaspoons sesame seeds, toasted

1. Combine first 6 ingredients in a nonstick skillet. Place over medium-high heat until hot. Add broccoli, and cook, uncovered, 8 to 10 minutes or until crisp-tender, stirring occasionally. Sprinkle with sesame seeds. Yield: 4 (1-cup) servings.

Glazed Brussels Sprouts and Baby Carrots

Glazed Brussels Sprouts and Baby Carrots

Time: Prep 12 minutes; Cook 15 minutes

³/₄ pound fresh brussels sprouts
³/₄ pound baby carrots, scraped
¹/₃ cup honey-mustard barbecue sauce
2 teaspoons grated orange rind
¹/₄ cup unsweetened orange juice
   Orange zest (optional)

Per Serving:
Calories 112
Carbohydrate 25.2g
Protein 3.3g
Fat 0.4g
Fiber 6.0g
Cholesterol 0mg
Sodium 272mg
Calcium 56mg
Exchanges:
½ Grain
2 Vegetable

1. Wash brussels sprouts thoroughly, and remove discolored leaves. Cut off stem ends, and cut a shallow X in bottom of each sprout.

2. Place brussels sprouts and carrots in a large saucepan; add water to cover. Bring to a boil; cook 15 minutes or until vegetables are tender. Drain; transfer to a medium bowl.

3. Combine barbecue sauce, orange rind, and orange juice; add to vegetables, tossing gently. Garnish with orange zest, if desired. Yield: 4 (1-cup) servings.

I've found that the sweetest brussels sprouts are small, bright green ones. Be sure to skip over any that look old, because they'll taste bitter.

Sugar Snap Peas with Papaya Salsa

Sugar Snap Peas with Papaya Salsa

Time: Prep 8 minutes; Cook 3 minutes

Per Serving:
Calories 68
Carbohydrate 13.6g
Protein 3.5g
Fat 0.3g
Fiber 3.9g
Cholesterol 0mg
Sodium 82mg
Calcium 67mg
Exchanges:
½ Fruit
1 Vegetable

1   cup peeled, seeded, and diced papaya
½   cup chopped fresh cilantro
1   tablespoon minced onion
2   teaspoons lime juice
2   teaspoons rice wine vinegar
⅛   teaspoon salt
⅛   teaspoon ground white pepper
1   pound fresh Sugar Snap peas, trimmed

1. Combine first 7 ingredients in a bowl; toss gently, and set aside.

2. Arrange peas in a steamer basket over boiling water. Cover and steam 3 minutes or until peas are crisp-tender; drain well.

3. Transfer peas to a serving bowl; top with papaya mixture. Serve immediately. Yield: 4 (1-cup) servings.

Roasted Green Beans and Onion

Time: Prep 7 minutes; Cook 15 minutes

- 1 pound fresh green beans
- 4 large cloves garlic, cut in half lengthwise
- 1 small purple onion, sliced and separated into rings
  Olive oil-flavored vegetable cooking spray
- ½ teaspoon dried thyme
- ¼ teaspoon salt
- ¼ teaspoon freshly ground pepper

Per Serving:
Calories 54
Carbohydrate 11.8g
Protein 2.5g
Fat 0.5g
Fiber 2.5g
Cholesterol 0mg
Sodium 156mg
Calcium 62mg
Exchanges:
2 Vegetable

1. Wash beans; trim ends, and remove strings. Place beans, garlic, and onion in a 13- x 9- x 2-inch pan coated with cooking spray. Coat vegetables with cooking spray. Sprinkle with thyme and salt; toss well. Bake at 450° for 15 minutes or until tender, stirring once. Sprinkle with pepper. Yield: 4 (¾-cup) servings.

Jicama, Corn, and Green Pepper Skillet

Time: Prep 10 minutes; Cook 5 minutes

- Vegetable cooking spray
- 1 teaspoon olive oil
- 2½ cups peeled, finely chopped jicama (about 1 pound)
- 1½ cups finely chopped green pepper
- 1 cup frozen whole-kernel corn, thawed
- ½ cup finely chopped onion
- ½ teaspoon ground cumin
- ¼ teaspoon salt
- ¼ teaspoon pepper
- 2 cloves garlic, minced
- ½ cup minced fresh cilantro
- 1 tablespoon capers
  Sweet yellow or red pepper halves, seeded (optional)
  Fresh cilantro sprigs (optional)

Per Serving:
Calories 100
Carbohydrate 20.1g
Protein 2.7g
Fat 2.0g
Fiber 2.2g
Cholesterol 0mg
Sodium 380mg
Calcium 29mg
Exchanges:
½ Grain
2 Vegetable

1. Coat a large nonstick skillet with cooking spray; add oil. Place over medium-high heat until hot. Add jicama and next 7 ingredients; sauté 5 minutes or until crisp-tender. Add ½ cup cilantro and capers; stir well. If desired, spoon into pepper halves, and garnish with cilantro sprigs. Yield: 4 (¾-cup) servings.

Maple-Roasted Squash and Pumpkin

Maple-Roasted Squash and Pumpkin

Time: Prep 10 minutes; Cook 45 minutes

Per Serving:
Calories 132
Carbohydrate 28.9g
Protein 1.6g
Fat 2.4g
Fiber 1.9g
Cholesterol 0mg
Sodium 103mg
Calcium 54mg
Exchanges:
1½ Grain

1   large acorn squash (about 1¾ pounds)
1   small pumpkin (about 2½ pounds)
    Vegetable cooking spray
⅓   cup maple syrup
1½ tablespoons margarine, melted
¼   cup sugar
¼   teaspoon salt

1. Cut squash and pumpkin in half vertically; discard seeds and membranes. Cut each squash and pumpkin half into 8 wedges.

2. Place wedges in a 13- x 9- x 2-inch baking dish coated with cooking spray; drizzle syrup and margarine over wedges. Sprinkle with sugar and salt. Bake at 400° for 45 minutes or until tender and lightly browned, turning wedges every 15 minutes. Yield: 8 servings.

Scalloped Potatoes

Time: Prep 15 minutes; Cook 40 minutes

1 clove garlic, halved
   Butter-flavored vegetable cooking spray
3 pounds red potatoes (about 6 medium-size), peeled and
   cut into $\frac{1}{8}$-inch slices
2 tablespoons margarine, melted
$\frac{1}{2}$ teaspoon salt
$\frac{1}{4}$ teaspoon pepper
$\frac{1}{2}$ cup (2 ounces) grated Gruyère cheese
1 cup skim milk

1. Rub a 10- x 6- x 2-inch baking dish with cut sides of garlic halves; discard garlic. Coat dish with cooking spray.

2. Arrange half of potato in dish, and drizzle half of margarine over potato. Sprinkle half of salt and pepper over potato; top with half of cheese. Repeat layers with remaining potato, margarine, salt, pepper, and cheese.

3. Bring milk to a boil in a small saucepan over low heat, and pour over potato mixture. Bake, uncovered, at 425° for 40 minutes or until potato is tender. Yield: 14 ($\frac{1}{2}$-cup) servings.

Per Serving:
Calories 115
Carbohydrate 18.4g
Protein 3.8g
Fat 3.1g
Fiber 1.6g
Cholesterol 5mg
Sodium 131mg
Calcium 70mg
Exchanges:
1 Grain
1 Fat

Chili Fries

Time: Prep 12 minutes; Cook 35 minutes

1½   pounds baking potatoes, peeled and cut into thin strips
1   tablespoon vegetable oil
2   teaspoons chili powder
½   teaspoon salt
½   teaspoon dried oregano
¼   teaspoon garlic powder
¼   teaspoon ground cumin

1. Combine all ingredients in a bowl, and toss well. Arrange potato in a single layer on a baking sheet. Bake at 450° for 35 minutes or until golden. Yield: 4 servings.

Chili Fries

Mixed Vegetable Grill

Time: Prep 10 minutes; Cook 10 minutes

¼ cup white balsamic vinegar
¼ cup canned no-salt-added chicken broth
2 teaspoons chopped fresh oregano
1 teaspoon minced garlic
1 teaspoon olive oil
¼ teaspoon pepper
4 (½-inch-thick) slices purple onion
2 medium-size sweet red peppers, seeded and cut into quarters
2 small yellow squash, cut into quarters
2 small zucchini, cut in half lengthwise
1 small eggplant (about ½ pound), sliced
  Vegetable cooking spray
  Fresh oregano (optional)

Per Serving:
Calories 101
Carbohydrate 19.4g
Protein 3.7g
Fat 2.3g
Fiber 4.8g
Cholesterol 0mg
Sodium 19mg
Calcium 68mg
Exchanges:
3 Vegetable

1. Combine first 6 ingredients in a small bowl, stirring well with a wire whisk. Place onion and next 4 ingredients on a baking sheet; brush vegetables with half of vinegar mixture.

2. Coat grill rack with cooking spray, and place on grill over medium-hot coals (350° to 400°). Place vegetables, cut sides down, on rack; grill, covered, 5 minutes. Brush with remaining vinegar mixture; turn vegetables. Grill 5 to 6 additional minutes or until tender. Remove vegetables from grill; cut onion slices into quarters. Garnish with oregano, if desired. Yield: 4 servings.

Layered Vegetable Casserole

Time: Prep 15 minutes; Cook 50 minutes

Per Serving:
Calories 80
Carbohydrate 13.2g
Protein 4.1g
Fat 1.6g
Fiber 2.1g
Cholesterol 4mg
Sodium 168mg
Calcium 82mg
Exchanges:
½ Grain
2 Vegetable

⅓ cup minced fresh parsley
1½ tablespoons grated Parmesan cheese
¼ teaspoon salt
1 clove garlic, minced
½ pound small round red potatoes, thinly sliced
   Vegetable cooking spray
1 cup sliced zucchini
1 cup sliced yellow squash
1½ cups sliced fresh mushrooms
½ cup chopped leeks
1 (8-ounce) can no-salt-added tomato sauce
¼ cup (1 ounce) shredded part-skim mozzarella cheese

1. Combine first 4 ingredients in a small bowl, stirring well.

2. Place potato in an 11- x 7- x 1½-inch baking dish coated with cooking spray. Sprinkle one-fourth of parsley mixture over potato, and top with zucchini. Sprinkle one-fourth of parsley mixture over zucchini; top with yellow squash. Sprinkle one-fourth of parsley mixture over squash, and top with mushrooms. Sprinkle remaining parsley mixture over mushrooms; top with leeks.

3. Pour tomato sauce over layered vegetables. Cover with aluminum foil, and vent. Bake at 350° for 45 minutes. Uncover and sprinkle with mozzarella cheese; bake, uncovered, 5 additional minutes or until cheese melts. Yield: 6 servings.

Soups & Sandwiches

Vegetable-Beef Soup (page 208)

Chunky Minestrone

Chunky Minestrone

Time: Prep 9 minutes; Cook 28 minutes

Per Serving:
Calories 187
Carbohydrate 29.1g
Protein 9.0g
Fat 4.3g
Fiber 4.1g
Cholesterol 6mg
Sodium 375mg
Calcium 223mg
Exchanges:
1½ Grain
1 Vegetable
1 Fat

2 teaspoons olive oil

1½ cups chopped onion

1 medium carrot, halved lengthwise and sliced (about ¾ cup)

1 clove garlic, minced

½ cup long-grain rice, uncooked

2½ cups water

1¼ cups canned vegetable or chicken broth, undiluted

2 (14½-ounce) cans no-salt-added whole tomatoes, undrained and chopped

1 teaspoon dried Italian seasoning

1 medium zucchini, halved lengthwise and sliced

1 (15-ounce) can cannellini beans, drained

1 (10-ounce) package frozen chopped spinach, thawed and drained

¼ teaspoon pepper

⅔ cup grated Parmesan cheese

1. Heat oil in a Dutch oven over medium-high heat. Add onion, carrot, and garlic; sauté 3 minutes. Add rice and next 4 ingredients; bring to a boil. Cover, reduce heat, and simmer 20 minutes.

2. Stir in zucchini and next 3 ingredients; cook 5 additional minutes. Ladle soup into individual bowls, and sprinkle with cheese. Yield: 7 (1½-cup) servings.

Sherried Mushroom and Rice Soup

Time: Prep 5 minutes; Cook 17 minutes

	Vegetable cooking spray
1½	teaspoons reduced-calorie margarine
¾	cup finely chopped celery
¼	cup chopped onion
2	ounces fresh shiitake mushrooms, chopped
2	teaspoons all-purpose flour
1¼	cups evaporated skimmed milk, divided
2	tablespoons dry sherry
⅛	teaspoon pepper
	Dash of salt
½	cup cooked long-grain rice (cooked without salt or fat)

Per Serving:
Calories 233
Carbohydrate 38.0g
Protein 14.6g
Fat 2.8g
Fiber 1.8g
Cholesterol 6mg
Sodium 337mg
Calcium 495mg
Exchanges:
1 Grain
1 Vegetable
1½ Skim Milk

1. Coat a large nonstick skillet with cooking spray; add margarine. Place over medium-high heat until margarine melts. Add celery, onion, and mushrooms; sauté 3 to 4 minutes or until tender.

2. Combine flour and 2 tablespoons milk, stirring until smooth; add to vegetable mixture. Add remaining 1 cup plus 2 tablespoons milk, sherry, pepper, and salt; cook, stirring constantly, until mixture is thickened. Stir in rice; reduce heat to low, and simmer, uncovered, 10 minutes. Yield: 2 (1-cup) servings.

Jenny enjoys Sherried Mushroom and Rice Soup by the fire.

Chicken Enchilada Soup

Chicken Enchilada Soup

Time: Prep 12 minutes; Cook 20 minutes

Per Serving:
Calories 225
Carbohydrate 20.0g
Protein 20.2g
Fat 6.6g
Fiber 1.5g
Cholesterol 38mg
Sodium 397mg
Calcium 136mg
Exchanges:
1 Grain
2 Lean Meat
1 Vegetable

1   (6-inch) corn tortilla
    Vegetable cooking spray
1   teaspoon vegetable oil
1   (4-ounce) skinned, boned chicken breast half,
      cubed
2   tablespoons all-purpose flour
½   cup no-salt-added tomato sauce
¼   cup skim milk
¾   teaspoon chili powder
¼   teaspoon ground cumin
⅛   teaspoon salt
⅛   teaspoon garlic powder
    Dash of ground red pepper
1   (14½-ounce) can no-salt-added chicken broth
¼   cup seeded, chopped tomato
2   tablespoons (½ ounce) shredded reduced-fat
      sharp Cheddar cheese
½   teaspoon seeded, minced jalapeño pepper (optional)

1. Cut tortilla into very thin strips; place on a baking sheet. Bake at 325° for 10 minutes or until crisp. Set aside.

2. Coat a medium saucepan with cooking spray; add oil. Place over medium-high heat until hot. Add chicken; sauté 4 minutes or until lightly browned. Add flour, and cook, stirring constantly, 1 minute. Gradually stir in tomato sauce and next 7 ingredients. Cover, reduce heat, and simmer 15 minutes, stirring occasionally.

3. To serve, ladle soup into individual bowls; top with tortilla strips, tomato, cheese, and, if desired, jalapeño pepper. Yield: 2 servings.

Italian Sausage-Vegetable Soup

Time: Prep 5 minutes; Cook 19 minutes

    6   ounces low-fat Italian-flavored turkey sausage
    2   (14½-ounce) cans no-salt-added stewed
          tomatoes, undrained
    1   (13¾-ounce) can no-salt-added beef broth
    1   (10-ounce) package frozen mixed vegetables
    ½   teaspoon salt
    ½   teaspoon garlic powder
    ¾   cup small seashell macaroni, uncooked

Per Serving:
Calories 147
Carbohydrate 21.8g
Protein 8.2g
Fat 2.9g
Fiber 2.1g
Cholesterol 15mg
Sodium 339mg
Calcium 46mg
Exchanges:
1 Grain
1 Vegetable
1 Lean Meat

1. Cook turkey sausage in a large saucepan over medium-high heat until browned, stirring until it crumbles. Drain; wipe drippings from pan with a paper towel.

2. Return sausage to pan, and add tomato and next 4 ingredients; bring to a boil. Cover, reduce heat to medium-low, and cook 5 minutes. Add macaroni; cover and cook 10 minutes or until macaroni is tender. Yield: 7 (1-cup) servings.

Vegetable-Beef Soup

Time: Prep 10 minutes; Cook 1 hour and 50 minutes

Per Serving:
Calories 79
Carbohydrate 9.0g
Protein 6.8g
Fat 1.6g
Fiber 2.0g
Cholesterol 13mg
Sodium 216mg
Calcium 44mg
Exchanges:
2 Vegetable
½ Lean Meat

½   pound lean boneless top round steak
     Vegetable cooking spray
1   teaspoon olive oil
1½ cups thinly sliced onion
1   teaspoon sugar
¾   teaspoon salt
1   tablespoon minced garlic
1½ cups water
2   (14¼-ounce) cans no-salt-added beef broth
1   (14½-ounce) can no-salt-added whole tomatoes,
     undrained and chopped
½   teaspoon dried thyme
½   teaspoon pepper
1   bay leaf
1½ cups coarsely chopped cabbage
1   cup chopped celery
1   cup sliced carrot
1   medium-size yellow squash, cut into 1-inch chunks
1   small zucchini, cut into 1-inch chunks

An added benefit to simmering a pot of soup is that it gives you time to yourself—time to enjoy a book, call a friend, or unwind from a busy day.

1. Trim fat from steak; cut steak into 1-inch pieces. Coat a Dutch oven with cooking spray; place over medium-high heat until hot. Add steak; cook until browned on all sides, stirring often. Remove steak from Dutch oven, and set aside.

2. Add oil to Dutch oven. Place over medium-high heat until hot. Add onion; sauté 5 minutes or until tender. Reduce heat to medium-low; add sugar and salt. Cook 15 minutes or until golden, stirring occasionally. Add garlic; cook 1 minute.

3. Add beef, water, and next 5 ingredients to onion mixture. Bring to a boil; cover, reduce heat, and simmer 1 hour. Add cabbage and remaining ingredients. Cover and simmer 25 minutes or until vegetables are tender. Remove and discard bay leaf. Yield: 10 (1-cup) servings.

Fresh Corn Chowder

Time: Prep 12 minutes; Cook 30 minutes

8 ears fresh corn
Vegetable cooking spray
1 tablespoon margarine
½ cup finely chopped onion
½ cup thinly sliced celery
1 cup peeled, cubed baking potato
1 cup canned vegetable broth, undiluted
1 cup water
3 tablespoons all-purpose flour
2 cups 1% low-fat milk, divided
2 tablespoons minced fresh thyme
1 teaspoon sugar
¼ teaspoon pepper
½ cup seeded, chopped tomato
3 slices turkey bacon, cooked and crumbled

Per Serving:
Calories 253
Carbohydrate 47.1g
Protein 9.7g
Fat 5.4g
Fiber 6.6g
Cholesterol 5mg
Sodium 275mg
Calcium 116mg
Exchanges:
3 Grain
1 Fat

1. Cut off corn kernels into a large bowl. Scrape milk and remaining pulp from cob, using a small paring knife; set aside.

2. Coat a Dutch oven or large saucepan with cooking spray; add margarine. Place over medium-high heat until margarine melts. Add onion and celery; sauté until tender. Stir in corn, potato, vegetable broth, and water; bring to a boil. Cover, reduce heat, and simmer 25 minutes or until corn and potato are tender.

3. Combine flour and ½ cup milk, stirring until smooth. Add flour mixture, remaining 1½ cups milk, thyme, sugar, and pepper to vegetable mixture. Cook over medium heat, stirring constantly, 4 to 5 minutes or until thickened and bubbly. Ladle chowder into individual bowls. Top with tomato and crumbled bacon. Yield: 6 (1½-cup) servings.

Fresh Corn Chowder

Apple Breakfast Sandwiches

Time: Prep 6 minutes

Per Serving:
Calories 236
Carbohydrate 36.2g
Protein 7.2g
Fat 7.4g
Fiber 2.7g
Cholesterol 13mg
Sodium 338mg
Calcium 77mg
Exchanges:
2 Grain
½ Fruit
1 Fat

⅓ cup grated apple
½ cup light process cream cheese, softened
2 tablespoons crunchy peanut butter
1½ tablespoons apple butter
⅛ teaspoon ground cinnamon
12 (1-ounce) slices cinnamon-raisin bread, toasted

1. Press apple between layers of paper towels to remove excess moisture; set aside.

2. Beat cream cheese in a medium bowl at medium speed of an electric mixer until light and fluffy. Add peanut butter, apple butter, and cinnamon; beat well. Stir in apple.

3. Spread apple mixture evenly over each of 6 bread slices; top with remaining bread slices. Cut sandwiches in half. Yield: 6 servings.

Barbecued Chicken Sandwiches

Time: Prep 10 minutes; Cook 30 minutes

Per Serving:
Calories 268
Carbohydrate 31.9g
Protein 25.1g
Fat 3.8g
Fiber 2.2g
Cholesterol 60mg
Sodium 446mg
Calcium 37mg
Exchanges:
2 Grain
3 Very Lean Meat

¾ cup chopped onion
⅔ cup no-salt-added tomato sauce
3 tablespoons sugar
2 tablespoons balsamic vinegar
2 teaspoons garlic powder
1 teaspoon celery seeds
1 teaspoon chili powder
2 teaspoons low-sodium Worcestershire sauce
¼ teaspoon salt
2 cups chopped cooked chicken breast (skinned before cooking and cooked without salt)
4 reduced-calorie whole wheat hamburger buns

1. Combine first 9 ingredients. Set aside ¼ cup tomato mixture.

2. Combine remaining tomato mixture and chicken in an 11- x 7- x 1½-inch baking dish, stirring well. Cover and bake at 350° for 30 minutes or until thoroughly heated.

3. Spoon ½ cup chicken mixture onto bottom half of each bun; drizzle reserved ¼ cup tomato mixture evenly over chicken mixture. Top with remaining bun halves. Yield: 4 servings.

Greek Salad Heroes

Time: Prep 14 minutes; Stand 30 minutes

¾	cup thinly sliced fresh mushrooms
½	cup thinly sliced cucumber
2	tablespoons sliced ripe olives
2	tablespoons crumbled feta cheese
1	tablespoon white balsamic vinegar
⅛	teaspoon dried oregano
4	cherry tomatoes, thinly sliced
1	clove garlic, minced
2	(2½-ounce) submarine rolls
2	green leaf lettuce leaves
2	ounces thinly sliced reduced-fat, low-salt ham
2	ounces thinly sliced cooked turkey breast

Per Serving:
Calories 345
Carbohydrate 39.3g
Protein 20.7g
Fat 12.0g
Fiber 2.3g
Cholesterol 58mg
Sodium 730mg
Calcium 107mg
Exchanges:
2 Grain
2 Vegetable
1½ High-Fat Meat

1. Combine first 8 ingredients in a small bowl; toss gently. Let stand 30 minutes, tossing occasionally.

2. Cut a thin slice off top of each roll; discard slices. Set tops aside. Cut a 2-inch-wide, V-shaped wedge down length of each roll. Reserve bread wedges for another use.

3. Drain vegetable mixture. Line each roll with a lettuce leaf; top with ham and turkey. Spoon vegetable mixture over meat; cover with bread tops. Yield: 2 servings.

Greek Salad Heroes

Mexican Chili-Cheese Burgers

Mexican Chili-Cheese Burgers

Time: Prep 10 minutes; Cook 13 minutes

Per Serving:
Calories 345
Carbohydrate 28.1g
Protein 36.3g
Fat 9.1g
Fiber 1.7g
Cholesterol 84mg
Sodium 655mg
Calcium 212mg
Exchanges:
2 Grain
3½ Lean Meat

1   pound ground round
1   cup seeded, chopped plum tomato
¼   cup minced fresh cilantro
1   tablespoon chili powder
2   teaspoons seeded, minced jalapeño pepper
½   teaspoon salt
½   teaspoon dried oregano
½   teaspoon ground cumin
¼   teaspoon pepper
    Vegetable cooking spray
4   (¾-ounce) slices fat-free Cheddar cheese
¼   cup nonfat sour cream
4   (1½-ounce) hamburger buns
4   iceberg lettuce leaves
8   (¼-inch-thick) slices tomato
    Grilled sliced onion (optional)

1. Combine first 9 ingredients; stir well. Divide mixture into 4 equal portions, shaping each into a ½-inch-thick patty.

2. Coat grill rack with cooking spray; place over medium-hot coals (350° to 400°). Place patties on rack; grill, covered, 6 minutes on each side or until done. Place 1 slice cheese on top of each patty; cover and grill 1 additional minute or until cheese melts.

3. Spread 1 tablespoon sour cream over top half of each bun. Place patties on bottoms of buns; top each with lettuce, tomato, grilled onion (if desired), and top half of bun. Yield: 4 servings.

Note: Although we don't recommend eating them raw, fresh jalapeño peppers can be put on colorful wooden picks and used as garnishes.

It's best to use plum tomatoes inside the burgers; they're less watery than other varieties.

Turkey Reubens

Time: Prep 10 minutes; Stand 30 minutes; Cook 1 minute

- ¼ cup white vinegar
- 1½ tablespoons sugar
- ½ teaspoon celery seeds
- 2 cups shredded cabbage
- 2 tablespoons commercial nonfat Thousand Island dressing
- 4 (1-ounce) slices rye bread, toasted
- 4 ounces thinly sliced cooked turkey breast
- ⅓ cup (1.2 ounces) shredded reduced-fat Swiss cheese

Per Serving:
Calories 381
Carbohydrate 54.9g
Protein 29.6g
Fat 5.8g
Fiber 4.7g
Cholesterol 50mg
Sodium 656mg
Calcium 307mg
Exchanges:
3 Grain
2 Lean Meat
2 Vegetable

1. Combine first 3 ingredients in a small saucepan. Cook over medium heat, stirring constantly, until sugar dissolves. Place cabbage in a small bowl. Pour vinegar mixture over cabbage; let stand at least 30 minutes.

2. Spread dressing evenly over 2 bread slices. Arrange turkey evenly over dressing. Drain cabbage mixture, and spoon evenly over turkey; sprinkle with cheese.

3. Place sandwiches on a baking sheet, and broil 5½ inches from heat (with electric oven door partially opened) 1 to 2 minutes or until cheese melts. Top with remaining bread slices. Serve immediately. Yield: 2 servings.

Turkey Sandwiches with Berry Cream Cheese

Time: Prep 10 minutes

Per Serving:
Calories 270
Carbohydrate 34.7g
Protein 24.1g
Fat 4.3g
Fiber 1.9g
Cholesterol 43mg
Sodium 354mg
Calcium 99mg
Exchanges:
2 Grain
2 Lean Meat

¼ cup nonfat cream cheese
¼ cup seedless raspberry jam
1 tablespoon chopped walnuts, toasted
8 (¾-ounce) slices whole wheat bread
4 curly leaf lettuce leaves
½ pound thinly sliced cooked turkey breast

1. Combine first 3 ingredients; stir well. Spread 2 tablespoons cream cheese mixture over each of 4 slices of bread. Top each with 1 lettuce leaf, 2 ounces turkey, and remaining bread slices. Yield: 4 servings.

Note: The cream cheese mixture is also good spread on bagels.

Herb Chart

BASIL *clovelike, anise flavor*

•Use in Italian dishes from tomato-based sauces to pizza, in egg dishes, meats, pestos, salads, and vegetables (especially eggplant and tomatoes).

BAY LEAF *spicy flavor, vanilla scent*

•Use in soups, stews, meat or fish marinades, pot roasts, and with carrots. Bay leaves should be removed from dish before serving.

CHIVES *delicate, onionlike flavor*

•Use in cottage cheese, cream soups, meatballs, poultry, sauces, scalloped potatoes, tuna, and vinaigrettes.

CORIANDER (cilantro) *citrusy, peppery flavor*

•Use in guacamole, salsas, seafood dishes, vegetables, and in Asian, Middle Eastern, and Southwestern cuisines.

DILL *sweet, caraway flavor*

•Use in breads, carrots, chicken salad, chowders, cottage cheese, cucumbers, dips, egg dishes, fish sauces, peas, and yogurt-based soups and dressings.

OREGANO *pungent, bittersweet flavor*

•Use in Greek, Italian, and Mexican cuisines. Goes well with beef, clams, mussels, pizza, pork, and salads.

PARSLEY *delicate, celerylike flavor*

•Use in egg dishes, fish, meats, salads, sauces, soups, and stuffings.

ROSEMARY *bittersweet, piny flavor*

•Use in beef stews, chicken, fish, grilled meats, soups, and vegetables (especially cabbage and potatoes).

THYME *sweet, pleasantly pungent flavor*

•Use in chicken, egg dishes, fish, meats, sauces, soups, stews, and stuffings.

215

Determining Your Needs

To determine your calorie requirements, multiply your current weight by 13 if you are a female or by 15 if you are a male. This is a rough estimate; calorie requirements vary, depending on gender, age, body size, and activity level. For weight loss, subtract 500 calories per day to allow for an average loss of 1 pound of body fat per week.

Whether your goal is to lose weight or to maintain it within a healthy range, the Food Group Exchange Guide is a great tool for healthy eating. Patterned after the USDA Food Pyramid, the Guide is designed around a heart-healthy 20% of calories from fat, and it emphasizes grains, fruits, and vegetables as the foundation for nutritional balance. The number of exchanges for each food group listed below your calorie level is the number you should try to follow on most days.

Food Group Exchange Guide

Food Groups	Calorie Level						
	1200	1500	1700	1800	2000	2100	2200
Fruits	2	4	5	5	5	5	5
Vegetables	3	5	5	5	5	5	6
Grains and Grain Products	5	6	8	9	11	12	12
Milk	2	2	2	2	2	2	2
Meat and Meat Equivalents	6	6	6	6	6	6	6
Fats and Oils	2	3	3	4	5	5	6

Metric Conversions

Metric Measure/Conversion Chart

Approximate Conversion to Metric Measures

When You Know...	Multiply by... Mass (weight)	To Find...	Symbol
ounces	28	grams	g
pounds	0.45	kilograms	kg
(volume)			
teaspoons	5	milliliters	ml
tablespoons	15	milliliters	ml
fluid ounces	30	milliliters	ml
cups	0.24	liters	l
pints	0.47	liters	l
quarts	0.95	liters	l
gallons	3.8	liters	l

Cooking Measure Equivalents

Standard Cup	Volume (Liquid)	Liquid Solids (Butter)	Fine Powder (Flour)	Granular (Sugar)	Grain (Rice)
1	250 ml	200 g	140 g	190 g	150 g
¾	188 ml	150 g	105 g	143 g	113 g
⅔	167 ml	133 g	93 g	127 g	100 g
½	125 ml	100 g	70 g	95 g	75 g
⅓	83 ml	67 g	47 g	63 g	50 g
¼	63 ml	50 g	35 g	48 g	38 g
⅛	31 ml	25 g	18 g	24 g	19 g

Equivalent Measurements

3 teaspoons	1 tablespoon
4 tablespoons	¼ cup
5⅓ tablespoons	⅓ cup
8 tablespoons	½ cup
16 tablespoons	1 cup
2 tablespoons (liquid)	1 ounce
1 cup	8 fluid ounces
2 cups	1 pint (16 fluid ounces)
4 cups	1 quart
4 quarts	1 gallon
⅛ cup	2 tablespoons
⅓ cup	5 tablespoons plus 1 teaspoon
⅔ cup	10 tablespoons plus 2 teaspoons
¾ cup	12 tablespoons

217

Recipe Index

Almonds, Asparagus with Blue
    Cheese and, 194
Ambrosia, 62
Appetizers
    Antipasto Cups, 36
    Broccoli Quiche Bites, 70
    Crab Cakes, Louisiana, 82
    Dips
        Black-Eyed Caviar, 69
        Chile Dip, Green, 78
        Salsa, Southwestern
          Bean, 78
        Yogurt-Pineapple Dip, 79
    Kabobs with Yogurt-
        Pineapple Dip, Fruit, 79
    Mushroom Crostini on
        Greens, 80
    Mussels in Tomato-Wine
        Sauce, 84
    Pâté, Smoked Salmon, 69
    Shrimp and Scallops,
        Ginger-Marinated, 83
    Turkey-Spinach Pinwheels, 82
    Wonton Chips, Sesame, 80
    Zucchini Wedges,
        Baked, 81
Apples
    Relish, Holiday Cranberry, 62
    Sandwiches, Apple
        Breakfast, 210
Artichokes
    Beef, Burgundy, 58
    Mushrooms, Artichokes and
        Portabella, 193
    Pizza Milanese, 129
    Strata, Artichoke-
        Cheddar, 124
Asparagus
    Cheese and Almonds,
        Asparagus with Blue, 194
    Salad with Asparagus,
        Potato, 174

Bacon Dressing, Wilted
    Greens with Warm, 172
Banana-Chocolate Chip
    Pops, 113
Barbecued Chicken
    Sandwiches, 210

Barley
    Casserole, Vegetable-
        Barley, 188
    Salad, Barley and Corn, 176
Beans
    Chili Mac, Spicy, 131
    Green Beans and Onion,
        Roasted, 197
    Minestrone, Chunky, 204
    Pasta, Fresh Pepper, 135
    Pasta Toss, Southwestern, 133
    Pies, Mexican Vegetable, 125
    Pilaf, Wild Rice, 127
    Rice Casserole, Cajun Beans
        and, 126
    Salad, Mexican Beef, 178
    Salsa, Southwestern
        Bean, 78
Beef
    Burgundy Beef, 58
    Steaks
        Diane, Steak, 141
        Grilled Spicy Flank
          Steak, 138
        Kabobs, Beef and
          Vegetable, 139
        Salad, Mexican Beef, 178
        Soup, Vegetable-Beef, 208
        Stew, Harvest, 55
        Wellingtons, Individual
          Beef, 142
Beef, Ground
    Burgers, Mexican
        Chili-Cheese, 212
    Meat Loaf, Jerk, 140
Beverages
    Alcoholic
        Cappuccino, Cinnamon, 59
        Cranberry-Wine
          Spritzers, 46
        Mint Juleps, Frosty, 52
        Peach Spritzers, 86
    Citrus Cider, Warm, 88
    Coffee, Spiced, 88
    Cranberry Coolers, Tangy, 87
    Cranberry-Raspberry Tea, 39
    Currant and Raspberry
        Coolers, Black, 85
    Mocha Milk Shakes, 87
    Orange-Lemon Tea, 42

Blueberries
    Bread, Blueberry Loaf, 95
    Cake, Orange-Blueberry
        Streusel, 108
Bran Muffins, Overnight, 90
Breads. *See also* Cornbread,
    French Toast, Muffins.
    Blueberry Loaf Bread, 95
    Cheesy Garlic Bread, 99
    Cinnamon Crisps, 100
    Herbed Breadsticks, 99
    Popovers, Herbed, 67
    Scones, Cranberry-
        Walnut, 92
    Sweet Bread, Rosemary, 94
    Wheaten Bread, Irish, 96
    Yeast
        Whole Wheat Casserole
          Bread, 98
    Zucchini-Orange Bread, 96
Broccoli
    Casserole, Broccoli-
        Rice, 186
    Quiche Bites, Broccoli, 70
    Salad, Chinese Chicken, 181
    Sesame Broccoli, 194
Brussels Sprouts and Baby
    Carrots, Glazed, 195
Bulgur
    Tabbouleh, Southwestern, 174
Burritos, West Coast
    Breakfast, 120
Butterscotch Bars, 117

Cabbage
    Salad, Chinese Chicken, 181
    Slaw, Pineapple, 170
    Slaw, Spicy, 42
    Turkey Reubens, 213
Cakes
    Angel Food Cake with
        Caramel-Coffee
        Sauce, 106
    Cheesecakes, Individual
        Lime, 73
    Chocolate Cupcakes,
        Double-, 105
    Pound Cake, Pumpkin-
        Pecan, 107

Cakes (continued)
    Spice Squares, Autumn, 56
    Streusel Cake, Orange-
        Blueberry, 108
    Caramel-Coffee Sauce, Angel
        Food Cake with, 106
Carrots
    Antipasto Cups, 36
    Baby Carrots, Glazed Brussels
        Sprouts and, 195
    Beef, Burgundy, 58
    Maple-Mustard Carrots, 45
    Ragoût, Veal, 143
Casseroles
    Beans and Rice Casserole,
        Cajun, 126
    Broccoli-Rice Casserole, 186
    Potatoes, Scalloped, 199
    Turkey Enchiladas, 156
    Vegetable-Barley
        Casserole, 188
    Vegetable Casserole,
        Layered, 202
Cheese
    Asparagus with Blue Cheese
        and Almonds, 194
    Bread, Cheesy Garlic, 99
    Burgers, Mexican
        Chili-Cheese, 212
    Enchiladas, Turkey, 156
    Macaroni and Cheese, Baked
        Vegetable, 132
    Manicotti, Spinach, 130
    Parmesan Chicken with
        Tomato Cream
        Sauce, 152
    Pizza, Caramelized
        Onion, 128
    Pizza Milanese, 129
    Potatoes, Cheese-Stuffed, 136
    Potatoes, Scalloped, 199
    Quiche Bites, Broccoli, 70
    Sandwiches with Berry Cream
        Cheese, Turkey, 214
    Strata, Artichoke-
        Cheddar, 124
Cheesecakes. See Cakes/
    Cheesecakes.
Cherry Sauce, Lamb Chops
    with, 145
Chicken
    Breasts with Marmalade,
        Chicken, 154
    Drumsticks, Crispy, 156
    Garlic-Ginger Chicken, 153

Lemon Chicken and
    Potatoes, 155
Orzo, Moroccan Chicken
    and, 150
Parmesan Chicken with
    Tomato Cream
    Sauce, 152
Poached Ginger
    Chicken, 151
Rice, Chicken Fried, 148
Salads
    Chinese Chicken
        Salad, 181
    Grilled Chicken Salad, 33
    Peach Salad, Savory
        Chicken and, 180
    Roasted Chicken and
        Vegetable Salad, 51
Sandwiches, Barbecued
    Chicken, 210
Soup, Chicken
    Enchilada, 206
Vegetable Lo Mein, Chicken
    and, 149
Chili Mac, Spicy, 131
Chocolate
    Brownies, Chewy Coffee, 118
    Cookies, Chocolate
        Chip-Strawberry
        Thumbprint, 116
    Cupcakes, Double-
        Chocolate, 105
    Pops, Banana-Chocolate
        Chip, 113
    Shakes, Mocha Milk, 87
    Squares, Autumn Spice, 56
Chowder, Fresh Corn, 209
Coffee
    Brownies, Chewy Coffee, 118
    Cappuccino, Cinnamon, 59
    Spiced Coffee, 88
Coleslaw. See Cabbage/Slaw.
Cookies
    Bars, Butterscotch, 117
    Brownies, Chewy Coffee, 118
    Chocolate Chip-Strawberry
        Thumbprint
        Cookies, 116
    Molasses Crinkles, 115
Corn
    Chowder, Fresh Corn, 209
    Pasta Toss, Southwestern, 133
    Pilaf, Wild Rice, 127
    Salad, Barley and Corn, 176
    Salad, Zesty Corn, 49

Skillet, Jicama, Corn, and
    Green Pepper, 197
Tilapia in Corn Husks, 162
Cornbread Stuffing, Turkey
    Breast with, 61
Cornish Hens, Tropical, 159
Couscous
    Chicken Breasts with
        Marmalade, 154
Crab
    Cakes, Louisiana Crab, 82
    Cakes with Lemon Sauce,
        Seasoned Crab, 164
    Imperial, Crabmeat, 73
Cranberries
    Coolers, Tangy Cranberry, 87
    Relish, Holiday Cranberry, 62
    Salad, Festive Cranberry-
        Pear, 168
    Scones, Cranberry-Walnut, 92
    Spritzers, Cranberry-Wine, 46
    Tea, Cranberry-Raspberry, 39

Desserts. See also Cakes, Cookies,
    Ice Creams and Sherbets,
    Pies.
    Fruit
        Ambrosia, 62
        Crème Brûlée, Fruited, 102
        Peach Crisps, Quick, 114
        Pears with Raspberry
            Sherbet, Poached, 104
        Strawberries, Glazed, 52
        Tropical Fruit in Custard
            Sauce, 103
    Honey-Nut Phyllo Slices, 114
    Sauces
        Caramel-Coffee Sauce,
            Angel Food Cake
            with, 106
        Strawberry Sauce,
            Fresh, 102
Dressing. See Stuffing.

Eggplant Sauce, Mostaccioli
    with, 190
Eggs
    Burritos, West Coast
        Breakfast, 120
    Frittata, Vegetable, 121
    Omelet, Creole, 66
    Omelet, Herbed
        Gazpacho, 122

Eggs (continued)
    Scramble, Sunshine, 122
    Strata, Artichoke-
        Cheddar, 124
Enchiladas
    Soup, Chicken
        Enchilada, 206
    Turkey Enchiladas, 156

Fettuccine
    Parslied Fettuccine, 59
    Veal Ragoût, 143
Fish. See also Seafood.
    Mahimahi with Pineapple,
        Grilled, 160
    Salmon
        Pâté, Smoked Salmon, 69
        Poached Salmon with
            Yellow Tomato Salsa, 161
    Swordfish
        Herb-Grilled Swordfish, 48
        Mushroom-Tomato Sauce,
            Swordfish with, 163
    Tilapia in Corn Husks, 162
    Tuna
        Pita Niçoise, 38
        Salad Niçoise, 182
French Toast, Quick, 93
Frittata, Vegetable, 121
Fruit. See also specific types.
    Ambrosia, 62
    Cider, Warm Citrus, 88
    Compote, Minted Fruit, 65
    Cornish Hens, Tropical, 159
    Crème Brûlée, Fruited, 102
    Cup, Sparkling Fresh Fruit, 39
    Kabobs with Yogurt-Pineapple
        Dip, Fruit, 79
    Tropical Fruit in Custard
        Sauce, 103

Greens
    Mixed Greens with Balsamic
        Vinaigrette, 170
    Mushroom Crostini on
        Greens, 80
    Wilted Greens with Warm
        Bacon Dressing, 172

Ham. See also Pork.
    Heroes, Greek Salad, 211
    Tortellini Toss, 71

Honey
    Dressing, Honey-Mustard, 33
    Phyllo Slices, Honey-Nut, 114

Ice Creams and Sherbets
    Banana-Chocolate Chip
        Pops, 113
    Lemon Sherbet,
        Refreshing, 112
    Mocha Milk Shakes, 87
    Peach Ice Milk, Brandied, 34
    Spumoni Loaf, 111
    Strawberry Crunch
        Parfaits, 110

Jicama
    Salad, Citrus-Jicama, 168
    Skillet, Jicama, Corn, and
        Green Pepper, 197
    Tabbouleh, Southwestern, 174

Kabobs
    Beef and Vegetable
        Kabobs, 139
    Fruit Kabobs with Yogurt-
        Pineapple Dip, 79
    Turkey Kabobs, Glazed, 45

Lamb Chops with Cherry
    Sauce, 145
Leeks
    Ragoût, Veal, 143
Lemon
    Chicken and Potatoes,
        Lemon, 155
    Pie, Lemon Cream, 109
    Sauce, Lemon, 164
    Scallops, Lemon-Parsley
        Broiled, 165
    Sherbet, Refreshing
        Lemon, 112
    Tea, Orange-Lemon, 42
Lentil Salad, 172
Lime Cheesecakes,
    Individual, 73

Macaroni
    Cheese, Baked Vegetable
        Macaroni and, 132
    Chili Mac, Spicy, 131

Manicotti, Spinach, 130
Meat Loaf. See Beef, Ground/
    Meat Loaf.
Molasses Crinkles, 115
Muffins
    Bran Muffins, Overnight, 90
    Raspberry-Filled Cinnamon
        Muffins, 90
Mushrooms
    Artichokes and Portabella
        Mushrooms, 193
    Beef Wellingtons,
        Individual, 142
    Bundles, Mushroom
        Phyllo, 70
    Crostini on Greens,
        Mushroom, 80
    Heroes, Greek Salad, 211
    Sauce, Swordfish with
        Mushroom-Tomato, 163
    Soup, Sherried Mushroom
        and Rice, 205
Mussels in Tomato-Wine
    Sauce, 84
Mustard
    Carrots, Maple-Mustard, 45
    Dressing, Honey-Mustard, 33
    Sauce, Pasta Primavera with
        Mustard, 192

Olives
    Niçoise, Pita, 38
    Tortellini Toss, 71
Omelets
    Creole Omelet, 66
    Gazpacho Omelet,
        Herbed, 122
Onions
    Beans and Onion, Roasted
        Green, 197
    Pizza, Caramelized
        Onion, 128
    Salad, Orange and
        Onion, 169
Oranges
    Bread, Zucchini-Orange, 96
    Cake, Orange-Blueberry
        Streusel, 108
    Salad, Citrus-Jicama, 168
    Salad, Orange and
        Onion, 169
    Tea, Orange-Lemon, 42
Orzo, Moroccan Chicken
    and, 150

Papaya Salsa, Sugar Snap Peas
 with, 196
Pastas. *See also* specific types.
 Chicken and Vegetable Lo
  Mein, 149
 Chicken with Tomato Cream
  Sauce, Parmesan, 152
 Herbed Pasta, Creamy, 191
 Mostaccioli with Eggplant
  Sauce, 190
 Orecchiette, Garden, 134
 Pepper Pasta, Fresh, 135
 Pesto Pasta and Turkey, 158
 Primavera with Mustard
  Sauce, Pasta, 192
 Salad, Confetti Pasta, 177
 Southwestern Pasta Toss, 133
 Steak, Grilled Spicy Flank, 138
 Tortellini Toss, 71
 Vegetables, Pasta with
  Roasted, 189
Peaches
 Crisps, Quick Peach, 114
 Ice Milk, Brandied Peach, 34
 Salad, Savory Chicken and
  Peach, 180
 Spritzers, Peach, 86
Pears
 Poached Pears with Raspberry
  Sherbet, 104
 Salad, Festive Cranberry-
  Pear, 168
Peas
 Beef, Burgundy, 58
 Caviar, Black-Eyed, 69
 Greens with Warm Bacon
  Dressing, Wilted, 172
 Salsa, Southwestern Bean, 78
 Sugar Snap Peas with Papaya
  Salsa, 196
Pecan Pound Cake,
 Pumpkin-, 107
Peppers
 Antipasto Cups, 36
 Burgers, Mexican
  Chili-Cheese, 212
 Burritos, West Coast
  Breakfast, 120
 Dip, Green Chile, 78
 Green Pepper Skillet, Jicama,
  Corn, and, 197
 Meat Loaf, Jerk, 140
 Pasta, Fresh Pepper, 135
 Slaw, Spicy, 42
 Tortellini Toss, 71

Pies
 Lemon Cream Pie, 109
 Vegetable Pies, Mexican, 125
Pineapple
 Dip, Yogurt-Pineapple, 79
 Mahimahi with Pineapple,
  Grilled, 160
 Relish, Holiday Cranberry, 62
 Slaw, Pineapple, 170
 Spumoni Loaf, 111
 Squares, Autumn Spice, 56
Pizza
 Milanese, Pizza, 129
 Onion Pizza,
  Caramelized, 128
 Party Pizzas, 36
Polenta with Sun-Dried
 Tomatoes, 187
Pork. *See also* Bacon, Ham,
 Sausage.
 Chops, Red Currant-Glazed
  Pork, 146
 Roast, Peppercorn-Crusted
  Pork Loin, 146
Potatoes
 Chicken and Potatoes,
  Lemon, 155
 Chowder, Fresh Corn, 209
 Fries, Chili, 200
 Niçoise, Pita, 38
 Pizzas, Party, 36
 Pumpkin Potatoes,
  Creamed, 62
 Salad, Savory Potato, 46
 Salad with Asparagus,
  Potato, 174
 Scalloped Potatoes, 199
 Stuffed Potatoes, Cheese-, 136
Pumpkin
 Cake, Pumpkin-Pecan
  Pound, 107
 Potatoes, Creamed
  Pumpkin, 62
 Roasted Squash and Pumpkin,
  Maple-, 198

Quiche Bites, Broccoli, 70

Raspberries
 Coolers, Black Currant and
  Raspberry, 85
 Muffins, Raspberry-Filled
  Cinnamon, 90

Sherbet, Poached Pears with
 Raspberry, 104
Tea, Cranberry-Raspberry, 39
Relish, Holiday Cranberry, 62
Rice
 Casserole, Broccoli-Rice, 186
 Casserole, Cajun Beans and
  Rice, 126
 Cornish Hens, Tropical, 159
 Fried Rice, Chicken, 148
 Soup, Sherried Mushroom
  and Rice, 205
 Wild Rice Pilaf, 127

Salad Dressings
 Bacon Dressing, Wilted
  Greens with Warm, 172
 Honey-Mustard Dressing, 33
 Vinaigrette, Mixed Greens
  with Balsamic, 170
Salads
 Barley and Corn Salad, 176
 Beef Salad, Mexican, 178
 Chicken
  Chinese Chicken
   Salad, 181
  Grilled Chicken Salad, 33
  Peach Salad, Savory
   Chicken and, 180
  Vegetable Salad, Roasted
   Chicken and, 51
 Corn Salad, Zesty, 49
 Fruit
  Citrus-Jicama Salad, 168
  Cranberry-Pear Salad,
   Festive, 168
  Orange and Onion
   Salad, 169
 Greens with Balsamic
  Vinaigrette, Mixed, 170
 Greens with Warm Bacon
  Dressing, Wilted, 172
 Lentil Salad, 172
 Niçoise, Salad, 182
 Pasta Salad, Confetti, 177
 Potato
  Asparagus, Potato Salad
   with, 174
  Savory Potato Salad, 46
 Romaine and Strawberry
  Salad, 171
 Shrimp Salad, Curried, 184
 Tabbouleh, Southwestern, 174
Salsa, Southwestern Bean, 78

Sandwiches
    Apple Breakfast
        Sandwiches, 210
    Burgers, Mexican
        Chili-Cheese, 212
    Chicken Sandwiches,
        Barbecued, 210
    Heroes, Greek Salad, 211
    Pita Niçoise, 38
    Turkey Reubens, 213
    Turkey Sandwiches with
        Berry Cream
        Cheese, 214
Sauces. See also Desserts/
        Sauces.
    Lemon Sauce, 164
    Peppercorn Sauce,
        Creamy, 147
    Tomato Cream Sauce, 152
Sausage-Vegetable Soup,
        Italian, 207
Scallops
    Broiled Scallops,
        Lemon-Parsley, 165
    Marinated Shrimp and
        Scallops, Ginger-, 83
Seafood. See Crab, Fish, Mussels,
        Scallops, Shrimp.
Sherbets. See Ice Creams and
        Sherbets.
Shrimp
    Cocktail in Shells, Shrimp, 41
    Grilled Shrimp,
        Southwestern, 166
    Marinated Shrimp and
        Scallops, Ginger-, 83
    Salad, Curried Shrimp, 184
Soups. See also Chili, Chowder,
        Stew.
    Chicken Enchilada
        Soup, 206
    Minestrone, Chunky, 204
    Mushroom and Rice Soup,
        Sherried, 205
    Sausage-Vegetable Soup,
        Italian, 207
    Vegetable-Beef Soup, 208
Spinach
    Enchiladas, Turkey, 156
    Manicotti, Spinach, 130
    Pinwheels, Turkey-
        Spinach, 82
    Squash and Pumpkin,
        Maple-Roasted, 198
Stew, Harvest, 55

Strawberries
    Cookies, Chocolate
        Chip-Strawberry
        Thumbprint, 116
    Glazed Strawberries, 52
    Parfaits, Strawberry
        Crunch, 110
    Salad, Romaine and
        Strawberry, 171
    Sauce, Fresh Strawberry, 102
    Stuffing, Turkey Breast with
        Cornbread, 61

Tofu
    Chili Mac, Spicy, 131
Tomatoes
    Artichokes and Portabella
        Mushrooms, 193
    Marinated Tomatoes,
        Tangy, 49
    Pizza Milanese, 129
    Pizzas, Party, 36
    Polenta with Sun-Dried
        Tomatoes, 187
    Salsa, Poached Salmon with
        Yellow Tomato, 161
    Sauce, Mussels in Tomato-
        Wine, 84
    Sauce, Swordfish with
        Mushroom-Tomato, 163
    Sauce, Tomato Cream, 152
    Slaw, Spicy, 42
Tortillas. See also Burritos,
        Enchiladas.
    Crisps, Cinnamon, 100
    Salad, Mexican Beef, 178
    Turkey-Spinach Pinwheels, 82
Turkey
    Breast with Cornbread
        Stuffing, Turkey, 61
    Enchiladas, Turkey, 156
    Heroes, Greek Salad, 211
    Kabobs, Glazed Turkey, 45
    Pesto Pasta and Turkey, 158
    Pinwheels, Turkey-Spinach, 82
    Reubens, Turkey, 213
    Sandwiches with Berry Cream
        Cheese, Turkey, 214

Veal
    Ragoût, Veal, 143
    Sour Cream Sauce, Veal
        with, 144

Vegetables. See also specific
        types.
    Casseroles
        Barley Casserole,
            Vegetable-, 188
        Layered Vegetable
            Casserole, 202
    Chicken and Vegetable Lo
        Mein, 149
    Frittata, Vegetable, 121
    Grill, Mixed Vegetable, 201
    Kabobs, Beef and
        Vegetable, 139
    Minestrone, Chunky, 204
    Omelet, Creole, 66
    Omelet, Herbed
        Gazpacho, 122
    Pastas
        Macaroni and Cheese,
            Baked Vegetable, 132
        Orecchiette,
            Garden, 134
        Primavera with Mustard
            Sauce, Pasta, 192
        Roasted Vegetables,
            Pasta with, 189
        Salad, Confetti
            Pasta, 177
    Pies, Mexican Vegetable, 125
    Salads
        Chicken and Vegetable
            Salad, Roasted, 51
        Niçoise, Salad, 182
        Pasta Salad, Confetti, 177
    Soup, Italian Sausage-
        Vegetable, 207
    Soup, Vegetable-Beef, 208
    Stew, Harvest, 55

Walnuts
    Phyllo Slices,
        Honey-Nut, 114
    Scones, Cranberry-
        Walnut, 92
Wild Rice. See Rice/Wild Rice.
Wonton Chips, Sesame, 80

Yogurt-Pineapple Dip, 79

Zucchini
    Bread, Zucchini-Orange, 96
    Wedges, Baked Zucchini, 81

Subject Index

Balance
  for healthy lifestyle, 14
  in exercise, 22, 23
  of food choices, 14
Basil
  drying fresh, 20
  description of, 215
  using, 215
Bay leaf
  description of, 215
  using, 215
Bok choy, 149
Bouquet garni, making, 21
Breathing, techniques for
      deep, 25
Brussels sprouts, selecting, 195

Calories
  determining your needs, 216
  for weight loss, 216
Chives
  description of, 215
  using, 215
Cooking methods, low-fat, 15
Coriander (cilantro), 18
  description of, 215
  drying fresh, 20
  using, 215

Dieting. *See* Weight
      management.
Dill
  description of, 215
  using, 215

Eating
  pleasure of, 16
Exercise
  aerobic, 22
  benefits of, 22, 23
  mind-body component, 23
  moderate, 22
  resistance, 23
  stretching, 23
  suggestions for, 23

Fat
  low-fat cooking tips, 15
Food Group Box Guide, 14, 216
Fruits, seasonal, 16

Garnishes, 17, 20

Herbs. *See also* specific types.
  blanching fresh, 20
  chart, herb, 215
  cooking with, 18, 20
  drying fresh, 19
  flavored vinegars, 21
  freezing fresh, 20
  storing, 20
  substituting dried for fresh, 18
Hoisin sauce, 138
  substitution for, 138

Jenny Craig Food Group
      Pyramid, 14
Jerk seasoning, 140

Metric conversions, 217
Moderation, 14
  in exercise, 22
Muscle relaxation
      techniques, 25

Oregano
  description of, 215
  using, 215

Parsley
  description of, 215
  using, 215
Peaches, peeling, 180
Phyllo pastry, 142
Physical activity. *See* Exercise.
Portion control, 15, 16
Pyramid. *See* Jenny Craig Food
      Group Pyramid.

Rosemary, 18
  description of, 215
  drying, 20
  using, 215

Self-manager, how to be a, 12
Spices, toasting, 133
Stress, 24, 25
  preventing, 24
Stress-relief break, 24, 25
Stretching, benefits
      of, 23
Surgeon General's Report
      on Physical Fitness and
      Health, 22

Tarragon, 18
Thermometer
  techniques for using, 147
Thyme
  types of, 147
  using, 215

Vegetables, seasonal, 16
Vinegar
  making herbed, 21
  uses for, 21

Weight management, 12
  calorie requirements, 216

Acknowledgments

I am delighted to express my sincere appreciation to the following, who, through their contributions and own examples, helped communicate the message that diets aren't required for health and well-being.

To my husband, Sid, with whom I celebrate all the joys of life.

To Joe LaBonté, Jan Strode, and Dianne Mooney for creating a partnership between *Jenny Craig International* and *Oxmoor House* and for bringing to fruition the talent, energy, and experience to create a landmark book.

To Lisa Talamini Jones, R.D., of *Jenny Craig International*, for promoting the pleasure of eating as a natural component of balanced nutrition and a nurturing lifestyle.

Jenny and the cookbook team of Cathy Wesler, Dianne Mooney, Jan Strode, and Lisa Talamini Jones

To my editor, Cathy Wesler, R.D., at *Oxmoor House*, for communicating the beauty and ease of seasonal, low-fat cooking.

To the highly skilled test kitchen team at *Oxmoor House* who devoted hours to food preparation and taste-testing for this book.

To the photographers listed at the front of this book, with special thanks to Ralph Anderson, for the artful photography of food and its presentation, and to the photo stylists whose food styling highlighted the colors, flavors, and texture of the recipes.

To Teresa Kent, whose efforts infused a wonderful energy into this book's design.

To Colleen Hanna, Brian Luscomb, and Gary Wright for their skillful flexibility and follow-through from start to finish.

To all the team at *Oxmoor House*—Keri Anderson, Stacey Geary, and Catherine Ritter—for all their support back in Birmingham.

A special thanks to Ron Fowler for his gracious hospitality during our photo shoot.

And finally, to my dear friends, the Tuesday Group—Billie Koyl, Sonya Wilson, and Bettan Laughlin—who shared the fun of a ladies luncheon for this cookbook.